Tales of the CELTIC BARDS

Out of the Fire of Speech
Out of the Sword of Song
Out of the Well of Wisdom
The tales of the Strange Ones come.
Tell it from ear to ear
Let the Bright Knowledge run
As candle-flame among you
Til the tale is done.
Who enters the Tale walks the World between Worlds...

Tales of the Celtic Bards

Myth and Music

Claire Hamilton

BOOKS

John Hunt Publishing Limited
The Bothy, Deershot Lodge, Park Lane, Ropley, Hampshire, SO24 0BE
E-mail: office@johnhunt-publishing.com

www.o-books.net

U.S. office:
240 West 35th Street, Suite 500
New York, NY10001
E-mail: obooks@aol.com

Design: Andrew Milne Design

Cover illustration and frontispiece by Jane Brideson
www.magicalomaha.com

Cover design: Steve Eddy

ISBN 1 903816 54 8

A CIP catalogue record for this book is available from the British Library.

Printed by Digital Book Print Ltd. www.digitalbookprint.com

O Books operates a distinctive and ethical publishing philosophy in all areas of its business, from its global network of authors to production and worldwide distribution. This book is produced on FSC certified stock, within ISO14001 standards. The printer plants sufficient trees each year through the Woodland Trust to absorb the level of emitted carbon in its production.

Contents

Cymru

Armorica

About the Author

Claire Hamilton has written several books on Celtic and Greek mythology and the Arthurian Tradition. She also has an MA in The Bardic Tradition in Ireland from Bristol University and has performed with The Company of Strangers, a theatre group who specialize in giving bardic presentations of myths. She is also a musician, and has recorded several commercial albums on Celtic harp. She runs workshops on myth and music and is a member of OBOD, the Order of Bards, Ovates and Druids.
website: www.livingmyths.com

Acknowledgements

So many have inspired and helped with these tales, John Hartoch and Maggie Fitzsimons, my fellow performers from 'The Company of Strangers', Jane Brideson who caught the vision in the front cover and her frontispiece, Michael Mann who helped to birth the magic, John Hunt and, not least, my partner Steve Eddy who put up with days and nights of visionary writing when I became lost in the Otherworld. And lastly, the inspiration of the bards and druids themselves who travelled with me and spoke their secrets in my ear as I was writing.

A CD of music written and performed by Claire on the Celtic harp has been specially recorded to accompany the poems in this book. This is available from her website: www.livingmyths.com

Introduction

It is night in the forest. Low in the sky a slip of moon throws a pale light across the trees. In a clearing stands a grove of close-growing oaks, their great limbs hugged together like a circle of giant dancers. Tongues of smoke curl around their trunks carrying the smell of burning flesh, of fresh-spilled blood, and all the while strange sounds are heard – sharp imprecatory cries uttered by white-robed druids wielding rune-carved staffs …

Dark groves, strange rituals, spells, incantations, blood sacrifices, a pagan priesthood presiding over primitive and barbaric rites – this is the vision many people have of the Celtic druids, that ancient order to which the Celtic bards belonged. But where has this image come from? Who gave us this description of the druids? What ancient sources told us they were so fearful and barbaric?

Contemporary Classical Writers

The answer is that this image of the druids comes from classical accounts, particularly those of the Romans. Tacitus, Lucan and Pliny were a trio of Roman writers who lived during the first century CE and who all gave negative accounts of the druids. These three writers stressed the primitive and barbaric nature of the Celtic peoples and their rituals, and so successful was their propaganda, that the druids, the most powerful and revered holy men of the Celtic peoples, rapidly became discredited.

But there are numerous descriptions from earlier Roman writers, some of whom drew on Greek sources (now lost), which give quite a different picture of the druids. These include Strabo, Diodorus Siculus and Julius Caesar, who all lived in the first century BCE. A few examples from their writings show a much more respectful attitude towards the druids. Diodorus Siculus said in his *Histories*: 'They are of much sincerity and integrity.' Strabo in his *Geography* pronounced: 'The druids are considered the most just of men,' and Caesar in Book 6 of his *Gallic Wars* said:

> The two privileged classes are the druids and the knights. The druids officiate at the worship of the gods, regulate public and private sacrifices, and give rulings on all religious questions. Large numbers of young men flock to them for instruction, and they are held in great honour by the people.

This was inside knowledge, for Caesar had a close friend among them, a Gaulish druid named Diviciacus.

There are also much later writers who speak well of the druids. These include scholars of the Alexandrian school who, though not contemporary with the druids, nevertheless spoke of them with respect; and Diogenes Laertius who said their central philosophy was: 'to honour the gods, to do no evil and to practise courage.'

From these and other writings, it would appear that there was an alternative view of the druids, one that may have been deliberately suppressed at the time of the final subjugation of the Celtic peoples. The reason for this seems to be that the druid class was solely responsible for uniting the various Celtic tribes into a recognized people and so in order to break the power of the Celts, the Romans found it necessary to undermine the authority of their spiritual leaders.

Yet, if the druids were as sophisticated as these descriptions suggest, why do we have so little firsthand evidence of them? Why do we have to rely on the biased writings of classical authors? Why haven't the Celtic peoples left us their own written accounts? Caesar is the only one to give us an answer, saying that the druids considered it 'improper to entrust their studies to writing.' He went on to offer two reasons for this, firstly the need to keep their teaching from falling into the wrong hands, and secondly their desire to preserve the exercise of memory.

Druidic Training

Druidic instruction was detailed and sophisticated. Caesar tells us that the full druidic training was long and rigorous, and could take up to twenty years to perfect. He also says that the most illustrious druid colleges were in Britain and that students from Gaul were encouraged to come to Britain for instruction. From other sources we learn that the training was composed of three main stages, those of the Bard, the Vate *(Vartay)* and the fully-fledged druid. Strabo gave a brief summary of the three orders:

> The Bards are singers and poets, the Vates diviners and natural philosophers, while the Druids, in addition to natural philosophy, study also moral philosophy.

But the three orders were evidently very closely connected because both Diodorus and Lucan speak of the bards and druids as if they were interchangeable.

The Bardic Order

Bardic training formed the core of druidic teaching. Caesar says it took twelve years, and involved huge feats of composition and memorising. Besides numerous poems, the candidate was required to learn three hundred and fifty stories, to study poetic form and grammar, learn the Law of Privileges, and compose *Dindsenchas*, or 'histories of place'. Such composition was achieved through sensory deprivation. The trainee bards were made to lie on the cold floor of a stone cell in complete darkness for a day and night, with a heavy stone laid on their chests to prevent them falling asleep.

The power of the 'word' in poetic inspiration was considered to be divine. Rhyme and rhythm were believed to hold a spell-like magic. By means of their verses, the bards had the ability to pronounce blessings or curses, and were greatly respected by the Celtic peoples. Their power of satire was particularly feared and was even used against kings. (An example of this is given in Irish myth when Corpry the bard, feeling insulted by his host, King Bres, composed a satire which raised boils on the king's face, forcing him into temporary abdication.)

Although writing was forbidden in the bardic training, the bards were taught an ancient runic script known as ogham (pronounced o'am). This consisted of a series of short horizontal lines attached to a vertical line – the number and position of the lines representing different letters of the alphabet. Robert Graves believed that ogham was also an encrypted code relating to trees, birds or animals. Examples of ogham script can still be found on standing stones.

Bardic Harps

Besides poetry, musical instruction also played a large part in the bardic training. Diodorus Siculus spoke of the bards as 'lyric poets' who 'sing to the accompaniment of instruments resembling lyres, sometimes a eulogy and sometimes a satire.' These lyre-like instruments were doubtless ancient 'clarsachs' or small harps. Harps had been around in various forms since ancient times and are believed to have been inspired by the hunting bow with its one string, which twanged melodiously when plucked. Early Egyptian harps (some of which still exist) were bow-shaped and sometimes strung with as many as eighteen strings. The earliest depictions of Celtic harpers, such as those found on stone monuments and crosses, show them playing both triangular and four-sided harps, and in the myths, the Dagda's Harp is described as a 'four-angled frame of harmony' (see 'The Three Noble Strains'). It is believed that these early harps were strung with either twisted animal gut or brass.

The earliest surviving harps in the west are the Brian Boru harp at Trinity College in Dublin, and the Queen Mary harp in Edinburgh. Although dating from mediaeval times, they were evidently modelled on much earlier harps. The Brian Boru harp, named after a tenth-century Irish chieftain, stands about three feet high, has twenty-nine strings, a curved pillar decorated with a double-headed fish, and a stout soundboard heavily carved with Celtic patterns. At the top of the pillar are two large settings for precious stones.

Bardic Music

According to Celtic myth, locked into the harp was the powerful music of the faerie people, the Tuatha de Danann. Their music was divided into three modes, each of which had an irresistible effect on the listener. These were the *goltrai,* the bitter mode, the *gantrai,* the joy mode and the *suantrai,* the sleep mode (see 'The Three Noble Strains'). One story relates how the great god, the Dagda, overcame his enemy by playing these modes on his harp and throwing them into uncontrollable states of emotion. It is also claimed in Irish myth that on one occasion the *goltrai,* or bitter mode, stirred the listeners so deeply that twelve of them afterwards died of grief.

Although these modes belong to the Irish tradition, there are hints that similar modes were used in Wales. The Welsh word *gan,* meaning 'song', suggests links with the g*antrai,* or joy-mode, while the Welsh '*suogan*' or 'lullaby' may derive from the *suantrai,* or sleep mode. As regards the grief mode, there is a mediaeval manuscript of ancient Welsh harp music written in triangular notation, which is believed to contain early bardic melodies. One of these was composed for the funeral of Ivan the Smith using the 'bragod-gywair' or 'bitter-sweet' mode. In spite of the guesswork involved in its reconstruction, the insistent and unfamiliar harmonies of this music make it one of the strangest and most poignant pieces ever heard (CD Track 3).

Harp Techniques

The instructions given in this manuscript (known as the *Penllyn*) demonstrate some of the complexities involved in traditional harp playing. It seems that the melodies were heavily ornamented and required the use of either the nail or the finger-ends for fast repeated notes. It is believed that, as with harp technique today, only four fingers of each hand were used, the little finger being too short to reach the strings. Harps also varied in size in Celtic times, being either held on the lap or leaned back against the shoulder, the hands being placed on either side of the strings. Although comparatively small, a variety of sounds could be produced on the instrument such as playing low down and close to the soundboard for a short tight sound or playing in the middle of the strings for a melodious sound. Because the instruments were diatonic, i.e. had no system of blades to create 'chromatic' or half-notes, it is believed that a technique of pushing against the top of the strings may have been used for this purpose. Added to this, special effects could be achieved such as strumming with the back of the nails or stopping the strings to produce a bell-like sound known today as a 'harmonic'.

Bardic Storytelling

Because of the emphasis on poetry and memorization, it is believed that in their storytelling, the bards punctuated their narratives with set poetic pieces. It seems likely that these set pieces were accompanied by harp and were keenly anticipated by the audience, rather like operatic arias today. Because of the importance of the three modes, it is not unreasonable to speculate that instrumental pieces employing these modes would have been played at dramatic moments in the stories, such as victory after battle or the death of a chieftain. We know from the myths and classical writings that although in the main the bards accompanied their own storytelling, some druids were in the habit of using specialist bards to accompany their stories. This suggests that some pupils of the druidic colleges may have chosen to specialize in the bardic arts and become travelling minstrels. Pupils who wished to continue their training, however, usually progressed to the second druidic order, that of the Vate (sometimes misnamed Ovate).

The Order of Vate

The Vate was a prophet or seer, known in Ireland as a *fili*. Besides Strabo's description of them as 'diviners and natural philosophers' we have that of Ammianus who said they 'investigated the sublime and attempted to explain the secret laws of nature.' The Vates were therefore searchers after occult mysteries. They were also professional seers who used methods of divination inspired by dream, touch and poetic composition. In this respect it is interesting to note that Caesar says of his friend, the Gaulish druid

Diviciacus: 'he claimed to have that knowledge of nature which the Greeks call 'physiologia' and he used to make predictions, sometimes by means of augury and sometimes by means of conjecture.' From this we can deduce that augury and divination were functions of the full druidic office.

The Vates were also doctors or healers, and studied the properties of herbs for use as medicines. Pliny tells us the druids used the selago plant to ward off fatalities and that they used its smoke to prevent eye diseases. More famously, he describes a ceremony in which a druid climbed an oak tree and culled the mistletoe with a golden sickle. As a gift of the sky-god, mistletoe was believed to have magical properties. It was used in healing and as an antidote to poison.

Because the myths are full of tales of shape-changing, it has been suggested that some Vates developed shamanic powers, being able to take on the nature of birds or animals and to travel to the Otherworld (see below). Such travel would require detachment from ordinary life. Thus, as with the bardic order, there were doubtless those who chose to develop their shamanic and prophetic powers rather than completing the full druidic training.

Druids

Whereas the Vates were primarily seers and magic men, living on the borders of the spiritual world, the fully-fledged druids seem to have held a more secular position in Celtic society. Caesar says: 'The Druids officiate at the worship of the gods, regulate public and private sacrifices and give rulings on all religious questions.' He also said: 'they act as judges in practically all disputes whether between tribes or between individuals.'

In their capacity as judges, the druids were known as Brehons. They travelled round the country settling claims and advising on matters such as boundary disputes and murder trials. They were expected to preside over executions and to determine and mete out appropriate punishments. Every three years they attended a counsel at the Festival of Tara during which the Brehon laws were discussed and revised.

As advisors to kings, the druids were required to give both spiritual and secular advice and also to preside at ceremonial occasions, such as ritual sacrifices and the culling of the mistletoe. The word 'druid' means 'Knowledge of the Oak', and it seems that most of their ceremonies were held in sacred oak groves. Caesar says that the harshest penalty the druids could impose was to ban a tribe or individual from attending such ceremonies. Caesar also tells us that the Celts were not afraid of death because of their belief in the Otherworld. It seems, therefore, that the druidic ban on attending ritual was considered a punishment worse than death because it prevented the offender from entering the Otherworld. It is important to see the druidic practice of human sacrifice in this context.

DRUIDIC SACRIFICE

The fact that the druids officiated at ritual sacrifices of animals is undisputed. An obvious example is the sacrifice of two white bulls at the ceremony of the culling of the mistletoe. The descriptions of human sacrifice given in Roman writings, however, may be overstated. For, while the Romans made much of the practice of human sacrifice at the time of the demise of the druids, earlier and more impartial observers give interesting qualifications to this custom. For example, Caesar says:

> … those who are suffering from serious illness or are in the midst of the dangers of battle, either put to death human beings as sacrificial victims or take a vow to do so, and the druids take part in these sacrifices … They believe that the immortal gods delight more in the slaughter of those taken in theft or brigandage or some crime, but when the supply of that kind runs short they descend even to the sacrifice of the innocent.

This would suggest that, for the Celts, death was as much a kind of punishment or atonement for crime, as an appeasement to the gods. Although there can be little doubt that human sacrifices took place, the context and frequency of the practice is not known. In this respect, archaeological evidence is also uncertain, the main evidence resting on bog bodies, like that of Lindow Man, which bear marks of ritual killing. In most other cases, marks of violence can as easily be attributed to death in battle. There is also no mention of human sacrifice in the myths. In a proper evaluation of the druids, therefore, perhaps less emphasis should be put on this practice and more on their other druidic functions.

Druid Philosophy

Besides being judges, the most distinctive role of the druids seems to have been as philosophers. Pomponius Mela called them '*magistri sapientiae*' (Masters of Wisdom). But Caesar gives us a fuller picture, saying:

> They have many discussions as touching the stars and their movements, the size of the universe and of the earth, the order of nature, the strength and powers of the immortal gods, and hand down their lore to the young men.

It appears, therefore, that the druids were well known for their philosophising. In fact, several classical writers even claimed that the druidic philosophy came from Pythagoras. For example, Hippolytus wrote: The Celtic druids applied themselves thoroughly to the Pythagorean philosophy ... and the Celts believe in their druids as seers and prophets because they can foretell certain events by the Pythagorean reckoning and calculations.' And Diodorus Siculus said: 'The Pythagorean doctrine prevails among them.'

Such assertions certainly give the Celtic scholar pause for thought, for they suggest that the druids, far from being primitive nature worshippers, were privy to the greatest philosophical thinking of ancient times. But one writer, Clement of Alexandria, went further and claimed that it was the other way round, and that the earliest druids had taught Pythagoras! He said:

> Thus philosophy, a science of the highest utility flourished in antiquity among barbarians, shedding its light over the nations. And afterwards it came to Greece. First in its ranks were the prophets of the Egyptians; and the Chaldeans among the Assyrians; and the Druids among the Gauls; and the Shamans among the Bactrians; and the philosophers of the Celts; and the Magi of the Persians.

This extraordinary assertion, formerly dismissed by scholars and sceptics, is now giving rise to new speculation as to whether the proto-Celtic peoples, the builders of Stonehenge and other Neolithic stone circles and passage tombs were, in fact, the originators of astronomical and astrological learning and that the druids were heirs to this learning and able to pass it on. Some of this speculation is based on archaeological evidence of extensive trade between the various Celtic peoples and those in the Mediterranean and beyond – for example, Greek vessels, Phoenician glass, and amber from the Baltic have been discovered at the early Celtic site of Hallstatt (see below). The freedom of movement between ancient peoples, and the dispersal of Celtic tribes across the continent was evidently more widespread than has been supposed, and supports the idea that an exchange of philosophical concepts could easily have been made. Thus the notion that the druidic teaching had either informed or been informed by that of Pythagoras is not a ridiculous one. The strong link between philosophy and music in either case is provocative. When considering the wisdom of the druids, it is therefore worth looking more closely at the teachings of Pythagoras.

Pythagoras

Pythagoras lived in the sixth century BCE and was the foremost Greek thinker in terms of philosophy, maths, music and cosmology. His teachings were secret and, as with the druids, he and his followers wrote nothing down. It was claimed that he received his wide-ranging knowledge from his travels in Egypt, Persia and Mesopotamia, and that he became an initiate of the Egyptian mystery schools, learned astronomy from the Chaldeans, received the secret teachings of the Babylonian Magi and studied with Zoroaster. From such teachings Pythagoras brought to the Greeks the idea of sacred geometry, a system in which number held the key to the whole universe and was expressed in music, hence the Greek system of modes and the 'harmony of the spheres'.

The Tetractys

Because he left us no written teachings, the knowledge we have of his philosophy derives from later writers, chief among whom was Plato. In his *Timaeus* Plato says that the most sacred symbol of the Pythagorean School was the Tetractys, a pyramidal structure containing the first four numbers which, when added together amount to ten.

X

X X

X X X

X X X X

The mystical properties of each of these numbers formed the basis of a holistic and philosophical view of the universe, which was highly developed by the Greeks and became the origin of much of western thinking. But even the briefest outline of such symbolism will immediately suggest similarities between the Pythagorean philosophy and early druidic beliefs and teachings.

The Monad

According to the Pythagoreans, the single point at the top of the pyramid represented the unity of the One – the indivisible, primary source of the cosmos from which emanated all creation. In Greek thinking, this number demonstrated that all the elements of creation formed a harmonious whole.

The druids also believed in the unity of the cosmos and, in particular, the interaction between the realms of matter and spirit. Druidic methods of divination such as the observation of the movements of clouds or the flight of birds rested on their belief in the interrelation of all creation. Also, the Celtic reverence for individual rivers, trees or hills reflected the idea of a single divine principle manifesting itself throughout all of nature.

The Dyad

For the Greeks, the number two represented the divisible, the root of all diversity, conflict and opposition. It was reflected in the great polarities such as life and death, good and evil, sun and moon. Plato spoke of this dualism as 'provocative things … impinging upon the senses together with their opposites.'

For the Celts too, the idea of dualism was essential in terms of understanding the natural world. Day and night, light and dark, life and death were respected as equal and opposite parts of the one whole. Rather than rejecting the dark and promoting the light, the druids acknowledged the necessary balance between the two. This is seen, for example, in the idea of the fair and dark faces of the goddess, which were equally revered. In fact, the Celtic respect for the balance of such opposites is shown by the fact that they counted their days by nights (as in fortnight or 'fourteen nights') and began their year with the season of winter.

The Triad

In Greek thinking, the number three was the first indivisible number after the number one, the source. It therefore represented harmony and completeness. The Three Principles associated with it were past, present and future. These principles are referred to in astrology as fixed, mutable and cardinal. Based on this triad is the Greek idea of the three Fates - Lachesis, Clotho and Atropos, who represent birth, life and death.

For the druids, three was also a mystical and spiritual number and was associated with the triple-aspected goddess. The idea of the three-fold goddess reflects the cycle of birth, life and death and the cycle of the three main seasons, spring, summer and winter. Throughout Celtic myth the goddess manifests herself variously in three guises, those of the Virgin, Mother and Crone. This idea also lies behind the Christian concept of the Trinity.

THE TETRAD

Being divisible and not mystical, the tetrad related to physical matter. The Pythagoreans therefore considered the number four to symbolise the mundane world. It also represented the four elements of earth, air, fire and water, which at that time were believed to be the four great pillars of the natural world. Alexander Polyhistor, writing in the first century BCE declared: 'Fire, water, earth and air – these change and are wholly transformed, and out of them comes to be a cosmos, animate, intelligent, spherical, embracing the central earth which is itself spherical.'

The druids also associated the number four with the realm of matter, and had a high regard for the four elements. They believed that the faerie race, the Tuatha de Danann, had once brought four sacred objects to their land. These were the stone, sword, cauldron and spear, which corresponded with earth, air, water and fire.

THE TRANSMIGRATION OF THE SOUL

Although the Tetractys formed the basis of his secret teaching, Pythagoras' most commonly known and most famous doctrine was that of the Transmigration of the Soul. By this he taught that the souls of men are immortal and live again for a fixed number of years while inhabiting another body. He also taught that between death and rebirth the soul rests in the Underworld.

Several classical writers have pointed out similarities between this doctrine and the beliefs of the druids. Caesar said: 'a lesson which they take particular pains to inculcate is that the soul does not perish, but after death passes from one body to another.' And Lucan said: 'They hold that the soul of a dead man does not descend to the silent, sunless world of Hades, but becomes reincarnate elsewhere; if they are right, death is merely a point of change in perpetual existence …'

But both Nora Chadwick and Miranda Green see a difference between the two doctrines in as much as the druids believed that the soul could only migrate to another human body, whereas Pythagoras taught that it could migrate between both animal and human bodies. They also point out that there are two kinds of belief discernable in classical writings. First, the transference of the soul between bodies, and second, the idea of a gloomy Underworld. The concept of a beautiful Otherworld existing alongside the mundane world seems to be exclusive to the Celts.

Archaeological Findings

Whether the druids owed their learning to Pythagoras or whether they produced an independent philosophy will perhaps always remain a matter of speculation. Nevertheless, comparatively recent archaeological discoveries seem to verify the assertions of the classical writers that the druids presided at ceremonies, practised astrology, revered the natural world and believed in an afterlife.

The first important Celtic site to be uncovered was the great cemetery at the village of Hallstatt near Salzburg in Austria. It was discovered in 1846 and contains some two and a half thousand graves dating from 700 to 500 BCE. This period coincides with the first phase of the Iron Age. The second great discovery made in

1858 was of a great quantity of metal votive objects at the bottom of a lake near La Tène in Switzerland. These objects are more refined than those of the Hallstatt period, and are decorated with the flowing motifs that are now so familiar to lovers of Celtic art. They date from 500 BCE and coincide with the second or Celtic phase of the Iron Age.

Archaeological finds from these and other smaller sites across Europe include bronze flagons and cups, chariots, drinking vessels, jewellery, swords and other weapons. More specifically, ceremonial objects such as crowns, headdresses, bronze staffs, wands, trumpets and golden torcs, or neck ornaments, have also been found. Such objects testify to the existence of a priestly class that presided at rituals. Archaeological finds of cauldrons and votive offerings discovered at the bottom of lakes provide evidence for the Celtic veneration of the sacred element of water, as do effigies of goddesses found in ancient wells.

A particularly important find in terms of the druids is the ancient calendar discovered in Coligny in central France. A bronze sheet, dated 1 CE and engraved with Gaulish characters, the Coligny Calendar combines both lunar and solar calculations and divides each month into fortnights rather than weeks. The months are marked either as MAT 'good' or ANM 'bad,' and it is believed that the druids used it to select auspicious days for agricultural and religious rituals. It is also believed that such predictions were based on astrological observations.

Another find is the Gundestrup cauldron discovered in a bog in Jutland and dating to the first century BCE. It is gilded with silver, and beautifully carved with images of Celtic gods and ritual scenes. It also bears the famous image of an antler-headed male figure thought to represent Cernunnos, Lord of the Beasts. But it has also been suggested that the figure could represent a shaman wearing antler horns. One scene on the Gundestrup cauldron shows men being dipped into a cauldron, and this supports the mystical idea found in myth that the cauldron had regenerative powers.

The Celtic belief in life after death is supported by the discovery of graves of warriors, chieftains and other important men and women. These are typically buried with artefacts thought to be of use in the next life, such as chariots, weapons, jewellery, pottery vessels, cutlery, cooking pans, cauldrons, wine amphorae and sometimes even joints of pork. This last is particularly interesting because, according to their myths, pork was a heroic and Otherworldly dish.

THE OTHERWORLD

In Celtic understanding there was no distinction between the Underworld, located beneath the earth and called *Annwn*, and the Otherworld, which lay either beneath the water or across the sea. The Otherworld was called by many names such as *Tír na n'Og*, the Land of Youth, Mag Mell, the Land of Delights and the Land of Women. It was a place that co-existed with the material world and journeys taken there were indicative of stages of spiritual development. Its proximity meant that visits could be made to it during mortal existence, but in order to travel safely, careful preparation and instruction were needed. The Vates were believed to be able to travel there and back quite freely because of their training.

Given the importance of this Celtic concept, it is not surprising to find that the characters in Celtic myth move freely between the two worlds and that the action of many of the stories revolves around bringing the characters into such a realm. Some, like Pwyll, are led to it by following threshold animals such as the white deer; some, like Cormac, are lured there by magical music, while others, like Oisin, are lured there by a faerie maiden.

For the untrained, however, such travel could be dangerous. The faerie men or women who came to lure mortals there were regarded with suspicion for there was no guarantee that those who visited would be able to return. In the story of Oisin, Finn mourns his son's disappearance knowing he is unlikely to see him again, and Oisin's eventual return to Ireland has tragic results.

Warnings of the dangers of the Otherworld are also found in the Scottish Ballads, especially those that deal with the Land of Faerie. Here, the abduction of mortals by faerie folk is a strong theme, as is the eating of Otherworldly fruit. Thomas Rhymer is warned by the faerie queen against eating its fruit because it would imprison him in her land, and Tam Lin, who fails to protect himself in such a way, has to undergo severe trials in order to return to the mortal world. At the same time, the tales themselves flicker tantalizingly on the edge between the two realms, enticing the reader to taste other realities.

Celtic Myths

Since the Celts were forbidden to write down their teachings, it is believed that they handed them down aurally using their myths as a vehicle. Ironically, after the demise of the druids, it was the monks themselves who decided to record their myths for posterity. Although the stories are believed to date from as early as the sixth or seventh centuries CE, they were not written down until the Middle Ages, when they were recorded in the vernacular.

The greatest body of myths belong to Ireland and a smaller collection to Wales. The Irish myths were recorded between the twelfth and fourteenth centuries, and the Welsh in the fourteenth and fifteenth centuries. The Scottish tradition has no myths to call its own since in Celtic times Scotland was linked with Ireland; nevertheless it has since laid claim to many of the Irish stories. The Breton myths were not recorded at that time but were handed down orally until the sixteenth century when some appeared in Albert le Grand's anthology of saints' lives. The rest were collected in the nineteenth century by Viscount Hersart de la Villemarque. (See individual sections and endnotes for further details.)

Because they were recorded by monks the myths have, understandably, been overlaid with Christianity. But many believe that, beneath this veneer, much of the druidic teaching still survives. In this book, the bards, seers and druids have been summoned to tell their tales again in the old way, using the magic of poetry, harp and music. Whether their knowledge comes from ancient esoteric sources or whether they were keepers of an independent spiritual tradition may never be known, but what is certain is that their myths are imbued with a deep mystical and spiritual understanding. It is therefore hoped that all who read them will be touched by their power, and will find in these ancient and Otherworldly tales both food for the spirit and healing for the soul.

ERIN

Erin is the Celtic name for Ireland and derives from Eriu, the ancient goddess of the land. There are three main cycles of Irish myths – the Mythological Cycle, the Ulster Cycle and the Fenian Cycle. Texts from the Mythological Cycle include the *Leabhar Gabhala*, or 'Book of Invasions,' which gives an account of various mythical conquests of Ireland. The Ulster Cycle concerns the stories of Cuchulainn, the great hero of Ulster, together with his Warriors of the Red Branch. The Fenian Cycle tells the heroic deeds of Finn mac Cumhail and his warrior band the Fianna.

The earliest Irish manuscript is dated 1106. It is known as the *Book of the Dun Cow* because it is said that St Ciaran originally wrote it on the hide of his favourite cow. This manuscript includes the famous *Tain Bo Cuailnge* or 'Cattle Raid of Cooley' which gives the exploits of Cuchulainn, and the *Senchus Mor*, which contains the Brehon Laws. Other manuscripts include 'The Yellow Book of Lecan' and 'The Book of Leinster', which were both written in the fourteenth century. Contained in these are the *Leabhar Gabhala*, or Book of Invasions, and the *Dindsenchas* or Place Name stories, as well as tales from the Fenian Cycle.

Prologue

The man with the strange eyes and the twisted hazel stick is coming to our village. Bruach is his name. We call him fili, for he is a seer and has knowledge of the hidden mysteries. For days we have been preparing for him and by the time he arrives the garlands will be finished and the meat tender in the pots. I have made a poem to greet his coming and practised speaking it to a few chords on my willow harp.

Although I am still a boy, I have been chosen to honour him because the people in my village think I have the second sight. I see things in visions that no one else can see and I hear voices in the forest that no one else can hear. My name is Magor, but they sometimes call me the Strange One. Everyone thinks that Bruach will choose me to follow in his footsteps and will send me for training at the Druid College. Half of me hopes for this and half of me fears it, for the training is long and wearisome and some of it takes place underground in the dark. For the bards have to lie still in their dark cells to make their poems, and place heavy stones on their chests to stop them falling asleep. They have to learn long stories of the making and history of Erin, of its tribes and conquests and all its great battles. Then they have to speak them to their harps. They must learn the strange language of signs and symbols called the Ogham because the word is so sacred that nothing can be written down.

All this I know, and I think I have already started my journey. I can play well on my harp. It is closer than a companion to me and understands my moods. I have learned the three great strains of music on it. I tried them on my mother. First I played the grief-strain, which made her cry, then, when I could bear her sobs no longer I played the joy-strain, and she immediately began to laugh. After that I played the sleep-strain, and she quickly fell asleep. So, although I feel afraid, I think I am ready for my destiny and I want Bruach to choose me.

There is excitement stirring and I think he must be coming now. We are all glad of his visit because he brings blessing to our village after the dark turn of the year. He comes from the great ritual of the gathering of the mistletoe, the beautiful white offering of the god, which descends upon our sacred groves. Bruach has been laying the white-berried branches on the Great Stone at the king's court at Tara where he presided over the sacrifices of the white bulls.

I know about this, for it is the holiest ceremony of the year and once I saw it for myself. But whether in dream or vision I cannot tell, for I was very young then, younger than I am now. It was early on a winter's day with only a beam of the sun's light, and a sickle moon alongside, or perhaps it was the sickle of gold I saw, for that was flashing high up in the oak trees, cutting the sacred plant with the white berries. All the while cries went up, chanting and invocations. And I saw the holy ones, the filidh, holding the corners of a great white sheet, which billowed like a sea of foam when the branches fell in it. After that I remember the slaughtering of the bulls, their blood almost black against their white hides. And I remember the smoke that rose from the altar and the smell coming from it. All that seemed strange to me then, but I know now that we were honouring the sky-god and our Mother Earth, and their union on the oak trees in the sacred grove.

After he has helped with the sacrifices, Bruach begins his annual travels. First he goes to the villages near Tara, and tells his tales to those who live in the sacred heart of Erin. Then, just after Imbolc, when the snowdrops are appearing in the woods, he comes to our village. Knowing he is coming makes us excited for we long to hear his stories. Some say they are simply good tales of love and war and enchantment, so they just sit back and enjoy them, but others of us listen with our hearts as well as our minds and try to discover the mystical knowledge buried deep within them.

Ah! I can see him now, striding across the plain with his white robe flying out behind him like a sail in the wind, his hair wild and his harp-sack strapped to his broad shoulders. He is coming nearer. I must take up my own harp and begin my playing. Soon I will see his strange eyes look at me, and I will know ....

1
Cormac mac Art and the Faerie Branch

When Bruach arrived he was fed and taken into the rath to rest. After this a fire was lit for the storytelling and he came out of his hut and made his way to the clearing. He was wearing dark robes over a white undergarment, with a rust-coloured cloak over his shoulders, his wild brown hair streaked amber by the sun. It was then that I sang my poem to him. When I had finished, he stared at me with his pale blue eyes. Then he held up his branch with the golden bells and shook it as a summons so that those who were still approaching quickened their step while those already assembled felt the power of the sound as a blessing or incantation, stilling their minds to receive his wise words.

'As you all know,' he said, 'I travel this land by earth, by fire and by spirit. And the tale I bring you is from a place and a time and a glory that is gone. But I, Bruach, have seen it on my spirit journeys.'

Then, seating himself again, he took up his harp with the double fish-head on the pillar, the gnarled wooden neck and the egg-shaped jewels set into it, and struck its strings with his fingernails so that the spell of listening fell upon the whole crowd. Then he began:

I have come from the sacred hill of Tara where lies the court of the High King, Cormac mac Art. It was he who raised the great hall and the buildings round it, he also who made the embankment and constructed the stout walls to protect it. And it is he who holds judgement there every third year, upholding and revising the laws of our land in consultation with its foremost druids and lawgivers. It is from such an assembly that I have come, and for those of you who have never seen this Hall, let me tell you of its size and splendour. The Royal Hall can hold a full thousand warriors and men of learning, each man seated against the wall with his shield hanging above him. Down the centre of the hall three fires burn, their flame-light dancing on the faces of the company and glittering on the shield-rows. The King himself sits at the southern end with the chief of the warriors and nobles about him, while those less worthy are placed along the northern end. This is how they sit by day while they debate the problems of government of this realm and also how they sit at night while food is brought to them and bards and harpers entertain them.

Now the tale I have for you happened many years ago and concerns King Cormac who will surely be known hereafter as the greatest king of all Erin. But if you desire me first to tell you the look of him, I can say that he is as fair as a man can be, perfect in form and utterly unblemished – as a king must be. His hair is golden and flows with a slight curl, he wears a red buckler studded with gold stars and animals, he has a gold torque around his neck and on his shoulders a full red cloak held with a clasp of precious stones. His shoes are fastened with buckles of gold and he carries two spears set with gold and red bronze. He is fair both in form and in judgement, and well known for his wisdom – a wisdom given him by the gods. But this I think you know, for his fame is great. But the story of how he came by it you may not know, and it is this story that I shall tell you now.

Taking up his harp again, Bruach drew from it a soft and languorous music after which he began his story:

Rising at dawn one day, Cormac looked out from the Great Hall and saw a strange sight. Before him on the green stood a tall, silver-haired warrior clothed in a long cloak that shimmered like a web of coloured light, and on his feet were two blunt shoes of white bronze. The man shook out his cloak and Cormac saw that every colour of the rainbow ran through its shining fibres. But when he looked again the cloak was hanging to the ground in folds of purple and the king thought that he had only seen the momentary reflection of the dawn sky. In his hand the man held a silver branch with three gold apples on it. When he shook the branch the apples tinkled like so many bells. The music of the bells rose like a perfume in the air. It was the music of the *sidhe*, a music of forgetfulness, and like all faerie music, had the power to lure away a mortal soul. The music of the branch crept into Cormac's heart.

The king came down from his chamber and crossed the green towards the warrior. They saluted each other.

'Where are you from?' asked Cormac.

'From a land across the sea, a land which honours truth, where old age and sadness is unknown, and where there is no envy or pride, darkness or decay,' replied the warrior.

'Our land is not so fortunate,' said Cormac ' nevertheless will you enter into an alliance with us.'

'Gladly' answered the other.

So the two men made an alliance and afterwards Cormac asked the man to give him the silver branch. The warrior smiled at him.

'The branch is yours,' he said, 'if you pledge to give me three things at the time I ask them.' Thinking of his stores of gold and silver the king agreed at once and bound the agreement with a solemn promise.

A year passed. In that time the wondrous branch brought healing to the land, for when any who were wounded in body or in spirit heard its powerful strains, they immediately shed their grief and were lulled into a restoring sleep.

At the end of the year Cormac was dining with his companions when a soft music was heard and in came the silver-haired warrior. He leaped down the Great Hall as if the touch of the wave lay under his feet, and bowed before the king.

'Lord,' he said, 'I have come to claim my price.'

'Name it!' said Cormac.

'First,' said the stranger, 'I will take your daughter.'

As he spoke, he looked at the young princess sitting beside her father. Drawn by the power in his eyes, she stood up and, as if in a dream, began walking towards him. The king cried out, but he and all his company found themselves powerless to move. As they watched, the warrior took the girl and hid her beneath his cloak. Then he disappeared.

After this a loud lamentation went up from the people. Cormac quickly shook the branch to calm them and their grief subsided.

But a month later, the stranger came again, and this time took the king's son. Again the people cried out in sorrow and again Cormac soothed their grief and his own by shaking the branch. Then another month passed and the stranger appeared a third time and took Cormac's wife. This was too much for the king, for no amount of shaking the branch could assuage his grief. He put on his armour, called up his best warriors and set out in pursuit of his family.

As soon as Cormac and his followers left the palace, a faerie mist rose up around them and they lost sight of each other. They called out, but their muffled voices became confused and distant as the mist swirled around them. Then, as suddenly as it had come, the mist cleared and Cormac found himself alone on a great plain that stretched away in each direction.

He looked about him in wonder. Before him in the middle of the plain stood a great fortress enclosed by a bronze wall. Inside it was a huge castle, its walls pale silver in the sunlight. He looked up and saw a group of faerie horsemen thatching its roof with pure white feathers. While he watched, a gust of wind sprang up and a host of feathers lifted in the air and tumbled about him like flying wings. When he looked again the roof had been stripped almost bare. Yet the horsemen continued with their work, undaunted.

He went inside the fortress and came upon a column of smoke coiling into the air. A young man was feeding a fire with thick oak branches. Yet each time he threw a log on the fire, the tongues of flame immediately devoured it. Even so, the youth toiled on undaunted.

After he had watched the youth for a while, the king walked on, still marvelling at these visions. And now he heard the trickling music of a hidden stream. He followed its sound and in a hollow beside the palace came upon a dark well. It was fringed by nine hazel trees that dropped their nuts into its deep water. Five salmon lurked beneath the surface, their bellies speckled pink by the juices of the hazelnuts, and all the while five lively streams flowed out of it, making the music that had lured him, a music more beautiful and melodious than any Cormac had ever heard before. He went towards the well and saw a bronze cup chained to it. He dipped the cup into the dark water and tipped it towards his mouth.

The instant the water touched his lips it was as if a thick veil had been thrust aside. All the dark places in his mind and soul suddenly thrilled with light and in a flash of insight he saw the world both close up and far away. He saw the whole universe as a great web of delicate silver strands reaching from the highest stars down to the flickering fish in the depths of the ocean, running from tree to tree and leaf to leaf, from bird to bird, from breath to breath, from soul to soul. And the web was continually singing. It was pulsing with every small happening. Every event and every thought was running through it, touching and changing everything else upon it.

'So the druids are right,' he thought, 'when they say that everything is awake and alive and speaks to them. When they see a flock of birds in flight and say that from their shape and number they have knowledge of a coming battle; when they see clouds in the sky, and say that from their patterns they can predict the fortunes of a man. They *do* receive such messages, and they have the knowledge, after all!'

Bruach smiled as he spoke these words. Then he began to play a strange and haunting tune, like the music of the waters flowing from the well. As he played, the sounds came close and touched our senses. The soulful melody ran thrilling up our backs and made the tears start in our eyes. It raised in us a terrible longing, a longing that we felt could never be fulfilled, and yet there was a strange and curious sweetness to it. While he played, we listened as if in a trance, as if we had just drunk the waters of the well ourselves. A long while we lingered in the Land of Promise, until at last he laid his harp aside and went on with the story:

Cormac stayed at the well, marvelling at his revelation. Then he rose up like a man in a dream and went into the fortress. As soon as he entered, a tall warrior came towards him accompanied by a fair-haired woman dressed in clothes of many hues. They led the king to a marble pool and invited him to bathe. The pool was warm, heated by hot stones that came and went in the water as if moved by unseen hands. When he had finished washing, the king went to join the stately couple in the Great Hall.

As he entered he saw that the hall glowed with torchlight. Down its length was a long polished table set with silver plates and golden goblets, waiting to be filled. In the fire pit hung a blackened cauldron, but below it he could see neither wood nor kindling. As he wondered at this, the great door opened and a man came striding in, carrying an axe and a log. Behind him trotted a pig. The man came to the fire pit and flung the log down. He swung the axe and cut the log into four pieces, laying them underneath the cauldron. Then he struck the pig two blows to quarter it, and laid it in the pot.

'And now to light our fire and cook our meal we must each tell a tale,' he said. 'But unless the tale holds truth within it, we will not be fed.'

Then he offered to tell the first tale.

'Now my tale is this,' he said, 'that when a neighbour's cows came wandering on my land and I returned them, this was my reward – a log, an axe and a pig. The owner told me they had these properties, that if I chopped the log and the pig into four pieces, and if four tales of truth were told beneath the cauldron, then the pig would be cooked. And if you think that was a marvel, here's another. For the man told me that when the next day dawned, I would find both the log and pig magically restored. And that is how it has been from that day to this!'

As he spoke, flames of red and gold and yellow leapt up under the pot and a great steam burst from its mouth. The company went to the pot and found that one quarter of the pig was cooked to perfection.

Then the warrior spoke next. He told of unseen powers that ploughed his fields and harvested his wheat while he was sleeping, and that bound it up in sheaths and gave him bounty, even to this day. And the truth within his story, that the hidden powers of the earth give man his crops and feeding, made the flames dance anew under the pot and allowed the cooking of the second quarter.

'And now,' said the woman, 'let me tell a third truth.'

'Once I had seven cows and seven sheep. These were magical creatures, for the milk from the seven cows was pure and rich. Indeed, it was enough to feed all the people of the Land of Promise. And the seven sheep were as wondrous, for their wool was thick and plentiful and provided all the people's clothing.'

And the truth within her story, that the magic powers of the animals give food and covering, raised up the lively flames a third time and allowed the cooking of the third quarter.

Then the company turned towards Cormac.

'As it falls to me to tell the last tale, I will also tell a truth,' said the king.

'A silver branch of lovely music so beguiled me that I offered anything within my kingdom in exchange for it. But my promise was foolish, for by it I lost my dearest treasures.'

'If what you say is true,' said the warrior, 'and indeed it is, for the meat is cooked to perfection, then you must be Cormac, High King of Erin.'

'I am,' said Cormac.

As he spoke, the warrior stood up. A silver light touched his hair and ran down his shoulders like a shining cloak.

'I am Manannan son of Lir!' he said. 'It was I who tricked you on the green, shaking my magic branch to lure you to my land.'

The sea god shook out his cloak and its rainbow colours danced about the walls.

'And I will tell you the meaning of the wonders that you saw,' he said. 'The horsemen are like a man who gives himself to vanities, and so his life passes away like feathers on the wind. And the woodman is like a man who spends his energies too much for others and so his powers burn away. But as for the well from which you drank, that is the sacred place where Wisdom lies. Blessed by the precious Hazelnuts of Inspiration and the wondrous Salmon of Knowledge, it sends its five great streams into this world. These are the streams of the senses, by which alone men can understand such knowledge. And it was to drink of this well that I brought you here, so that your kingly rule might be enriched with Otherworldly wisdom.'

As soon as he had made this revelation, the doors of the Great Hall opened and Cormac's wife and children entered. They ran towards the king and greeted him with shining eyes, and great was their rejoicing at being reunited once more. Then Cormac and his family sat down together and ate the feast that was set before them.

While they were feasting, Manannan brought out a golden cup and laid it on the table. Cormac looked at it in wonder, for it had curious symbols engraved upon it.

'This is a gift to you,' said the god. 'For the cup has this property, that when a false story is told before it, it breaks into three pieces, while the telling of a true story will mend it again.

You may keep the magic cup and the silver branch, the one to give you wisdom and the other to give you music and delight.'

When the king and his family had finished eating, they lay down on couches prepared for them and went to sleep. While they slept Manannan gathered them in his cloak and, leaping lithely on the wave-tips, carried them back to Erin. When they awoke next morning they were lying on the grass before the palace at Tara with the magic branch and cup beside them.

Bruach stopped speaking and began to play his harp again. The music was of the sleep-strain, but he only played it long enough to soothe and ease us. When he had finished, he held up his branch with the gold bells tinkling on it and said:

This poet's branch that I shook before you to begin my story, is like the branch that Cormac was given by Manannan, and so it ensures the continued remembrance of that branch. And I tell you that Cormac's Cup, the cup that discerns between truth and falsehood, will be remembered as one of the great treasures of our land. And Cormac himself will endure in the memory of his people as a most rare Sovereign. For few kings will be able to rival him, gifted as he was in wealth, in kindness and in wisdom.

He stood up. 'And now may the blessings of the gods descend upon all who hear my story.'

So saying, Bruach the fili turned and went up the path towards the hut that had been put aside for him.

As for me, I took my little harp and went into the woods and started to invoke the gifts of the Well of Wisdom. I took a strong rhythm for my incantation and crossed it with a mode from another tuning, then I made the sound of the waters with my nail-tips, trembling them across the strings while I spoke the words of power:

Fish under wave
Eó Feasa
Land under sea
Tír Tairngire
Well under land
Conla's Well

Nine hazel trees
Imbas forosna
blossom and fruit –

bursting bright crimson

Five streams outflowing
Streams of the senses

Five salmon red-bellied
Eó Feasa
Inspiring the poets
Aios dana
Inspiring the poets
Aios dana ②

And after I had made the song a great longing came upon me.

2

The Magical Gifts of the Tuatha de Danann

Next day Bruach found me playing my harp in the woods behind my house. He sat down quietly on the bracken and waited until I had finished. I was playing my song of power about the Well.

'How do you know these words?' Bruach asked.

'I have heard another story once,' I said, 'about Connla being lured by a beautiful faerie woman to the Otherworld. But that Otherworld was an island under the sea and Connla's well was on the island.'

'There are many ways to reach the Otherworld and many places where the Well of Wisdom can be found.' Bruach replied.

I blurted out, 'I would like to go to the Land of Youth. I would like to be a fili like you.'

Bruach looked hard at me. 'It is a long and arduous training,' he said, 'and you may not be able to withstand it. Nevertheless, there is everything around us here to make a beginning.'

He paused, then said suddenly: 'Do you know what are the four magical gifts that were brought to this land by the Tuatha de Danann, the faerie people?'

I shook my head. 'The first was the *Lia Fail*, a great stone which stands in Tara. It is the Stone of Sovereignty. I have seen it many times, and once I heard it. That was when Cormac stood on it. As soon as he placed his foot upon it, the Lia Fail gave a great roar which echoed down the great hill and across the plains below.'

He picked up a small stone from the forest floor and held it up. 'Listen to the voices of the stones,' he said, 'for they hold the energies of the earth. They are your guide to the deep truths that lie at the root of the living world.' He bent his head and kissed the stone. Then, clearing a square space in the bracken, he placed it in the corner facing north.

After that he held up his yew-staff in such a way that the sun's ray fell full on it. He said: 'The second gift was the fiery spear of Lugh of the Long Arm. He was the god of shining light, the son of the Dagda. In the days of the old gods, it was said that whenever the spear of Lugh was thrown, it never missed its target.' He raised his staff up higher. 'Listen to the voice of the fiery spear, to the wand of the mage, and the staff of the druid,' he said. 'For they carry the power of the sun. Learn the lesson of the fire of the heavens, learn the wisdom of its rhythms as it waxes and wanes, take strength and power from the time of its waxing and rest and sleep from the time of its waning. And remember that it governs the lives of men and the death and renewal of crops in their seasons.' Then he kissed his staff and bent down and laid it across the cleared square so that its head pointed south.

Afterwards he caught a seed of sycamore as it fell and blew on it while it trembled. He said: 'And the third gift was the Sword of Nuada of the Silver Hand. It is the sword that came in the faerie mist with the Tuatha. It is the king's sword, which deals the deadly wound in battle. Listen to the voice of the sword, it is of the air and lends discernment. Learn from the sword and learn from the element of air in which it dances.' Then he placed the winged seed in the corner facing east.

After that he sent me to fetch water from a nearby stream, giving me a silver bowl he carried at his waist. When I returned he raised it up in both hands, saying: 'And the fourth gift was the Cauldron of the Dagda – the great chalice that feeds body and spirit. If the dead are laid within it, they revive again. It is the mystical vessel of regeneration and renewal for it holds the waters of life. Listen to the voice of the Cauldron, for it speaks of the deep knowledge of the death and rebirth of the spirit.' So saying, he bent and poured the water in the western corner.

He bowed his head and stayed a while deep in thought. Then, taking up his staff, he left the woods as silently as he had come. But I remained there for a long time, pondering on these mysteries.

3

The Three Noble Strains

Next day Bruach came again to the wood and listened to my playing. I was in a light mood and was trying a piece in the joy-strain. Bruach sat down beside me and said:

Do you know the power of the strain that you are playing?' I told him that when I played it, I had made my mother happy.

'And what of the other strains?' he asked. 'The grief-strain and the sleep-strain. Are you also aware of their power?'

Again, I told him that I had been able to make my mother weep and to send her to sleep.

'You should be careful when you play such music,' said Bruach, 'for the gods themselves brought it into birth and the power of it is such that it can unlock the seasons.'

When he saw that I looked startled, he laughed and said:

'Would you like me to tell you how this music came into being? If you knew that perhaps you would be more careful in your playing.'

Eager to hear his words, I laid my harp down on the grass. The fili said:

Do you remember the Dagda, who led the faerie people, the Tuatha, when they came here across the waters. He was their chief. He was like a giant for he carried a club so heavy it took the strength of eight men to lift. And it was he who brought the magic cauldron to Erin, as you know.

The Dagda was a strange-looking god, and there are stories that make him a figure of fun. But there are other stories in which he is seen as a great lover. In fact, the greatest goddesses of that time gave birth to his children. One of them was Boann, she who loosed the waters of the River Boyne, and it was by her that he had Aengus Og.

Now let me tell you a little about Aengus, for he is the god of love and therefore is important. And, whereas his father was large and swarthy, Aengus was slim and beautiful with white skin and tumbling locks of hair and delicate features. Some say that white birds flew around his head, listening spellbound to his music. For Aengus had his own harp and was skilled in playing. But even so, his harp was not as powerful as his father's. For his father's harp had very great powers indeed, for in it were locked the three strains and the seasons, as I told you.

Bruach smiled and uncovered my harp again.

'I need a harp to tell this story,' he said. 'And as I have left mine in my hut, will you let me use yours?'

'Of course!' I said at once.

'Ah, but will your harp allow it?' he said. 'We shall see.'

He laid his hand on the wooden neck and stroked its smooth curve. Then he touched the sinewy strings with his fingers. At once a breeze arrived from nowhere and gusted through them, sending up a gentle cloud of sound that hovered around our ears. Bruach waited until their tones had died away. Then he bowed his head and began:

It was during the second Battle of Mag Tuiread, which, as you know, was waged between the faerie people and the giants, and it was while the Dagda was setting about him with his great club, cutting a swathe through the giant enemy, that his harp was taken. As soon as he discovered it, tired though he was, he set out immediately to recover his harp, taking Aengus Og with him. Together they followed in the wake of the retreating army, journeying for many miles until they came at last to the great banqueting hall in which the defeated enemy were holding a feast.

Night was falling as the two gods approached the hall. Through its slit windows they could glimpse the dancing of the fire flames, and hear the noises of the men as they dined. They waited in the darkness until the wine had gone several times round the company, then stealthily they entered the hall. Before them on long trestles were roast hogs' heads, sides of venison, and other woodland game. Bowls of nuts and fruit were set among the platters of meat, and wine flowed into the large goblets. A harper played and the men were drowning their sorrows at the way the battle had turned against them and seeking to find their valour again in drink.

Giant shields hung on the walls, glinting in the light of the fires and tapers. Weapons lay in heaps with tongues of flame-light playing on them. High up on the far wall hung the Dagda's harp, the Una. Through the smoke wreaths they could see its curved outline, the proud jewel protruding from its pillar, the carved fish-heads touching nose to nose, the ogham symbols burned deep into its scarred and polished body. Locked within it was a powerful music, music that could command a man's emotions, music that could kill a man or heal him, music that could unlock the seasons, loosing the waters of spring to break the whirling ice of winter. Although the harp was silent, through the smoke clouds they could see the powerful spells quivering on its strings. In a sharp voice the Dagda called to it:

> Come *Daurdabla*, apple-sweet murmurer!
> Come, *Coir-cethair-chuir*, four-angled frame of harmony!
> Come summer, come winter,
> Out of the mouths of harps and bags and pipes!

At once the harp came to him, flying down the long hall with such force that it struck nine men dead in its passage. The Dagda took it in his arms and spread his huge hands over the strings. Immediately he awoke the first great strain of music, the *Goltrai*, the strain of bitterness. As the melancholy music flooded from the harp, all those assembled began weeping, mourning their defeat, the deaths of loved ones, the death of the earth itself in winter, the frost-bound hollows, the bone-branched trees, the snow-bleached gullies. The music led them deep into the darkness, to the wellsprings of grief itself.

As he spoke, Bruach set my harp into the bitter-sweet tuning and began to play on it a music of such melancholy that I felt a wrench of pain so great it was as if my very heart's blood was spilling out. As he continued playing, I began to convulse with such violent sobs that I thought I would die.

After a few minutes, Bruach changed the tune and the pangs within my chest died down. He stopped playing and spoke again, while I lay exhausted at his side.

Then the Dagda unloosed the second strain, the *Geantraí*, the strain of joy. And now the healing began, the touch of hope, the searching of new shoots, the trickling of streams like laughter. The thrilling melody pulled them into gladness and the thrust of love. The warriors drank from their cups and goblets and toasted each other, feeling their strength come into them again. The Dagda played until they could feel the earth becoming green, the crops ripening in the fields, and the heat rising within the earth as the sun moved high up the heavens, conquering the force of darkness.

As he spoke, Bruach played my harp again. And now I felt as if I had drunk a goblet-full of light, which shivered through me, touching every part of me. Never before had I felt so vital and healthy, so strong and invincible. But already Bruach was muting the power of this strain, calming its strong rhythm into a gentle lilt. He said:

Then the Dagda unlocked the third strain, the *Suantraí*, the strain of sleep. And now the warriors felt the touch of ripeness and harvest, felt themselves cradled in the warm arms of the sun with the hum of rivulets and streams rising in their ears and a satisfying fullness spreading in their bellies, until the sweetness of sleep overcame them.

While they lay in their trance-like slumber, the Dagda and Aengus Og stole silently from the hall and, carrying the harp of the three strains of the seasons with them, journeyed back to Aengus' palace on the Boyne. ③④⑤

Bruach laid his harp aside and sighed.

'That story is one of the jewels in my store,' he said.

And he began to say more, but already I was spiralling into the depths of my body where I lay cradled in deep and soothing darkness.

While I was still in bound in the darkness, I felt the touch of Bruach's hand and his voice calling me.

'Magor, wake up! It is not yet time to be joining the sleep of the dead!'

As I opened my eyes, he unwrapped a little pack that he carried on his leather belt and took out a cake of nuts and honeycomb. He gave me some and we ate in silence. As we finished eating, the loud cheeping of fledgling blackbirds filled the glade.

'Ah!' said Bruach suddenly. 'I have not told you how the Three Noble Strains received their names.'

Feeling restored by the honey cakes, I looked at him expectantly. He wiped the honey from his mouth and said:

'Remember I told you of the goddess Boann?'

I nodded.

'Well,' he said, 'there are several stories about her and in each one she seems to be married to a different man!'

When I laughed, he looked at me.

'That was often how it was with goddesses,' he said.

He began fastening his pack onto his belt.

'In this story she was married to Uaithne, the Dagda's harper and by him she had three sons.

Warming to his story, Bruach continued:

Now when she was giving birth to her first child, she suffered great pain and anguish for he was a large and troublesome boy and took his time to be delivered. When her son was put into her arms, Boann looked at him and said, 'His name is *Goltrai*, for in my labour to bring him into this world, I have suffered much grief and suffering.'

When she was brought to bed with her second child, her labour was much lighter and the child was born easily. She smiled afterwards and said: 'His name is *Geantrai*, for I had pleasure bringing him into this world and even now it gives me joy to look on him.' After that she had a third child, and this time in her labour she was overcome by great weariness and exhaustion. She looked on the child and said: 'His name is *Suantrai*, for he brings with him the need of rest and sleep.'

As they grew up, the three sons of Uaithne and Boann took on them the powers of the three great strains of music, and they became famed throughout Erin for the skill of their playing and the power of their music.

Bruach began placing my harp tenderly in its woollen bag.

'And this is how they treated their harps,' he said. 'They wrapped them in three covers for protection. The outer covering was made of otter skins fastened with tongues of Parthian leather and studded with gold and silver ornaments. The inner covering was made of white kidskin, and within that was a layer of fine linen that was wrapped round the strings themselves. When they took their harps out, those who saw them were amazed. For the harps were carved out of rich wood inlaid with decorations of gold, silver and white bronze. Also there were gold figures of animals carved on them in such a way that when the strings quivered after being plucked, the animals seemed to move magically around them.'

Bruach tied up the woollen bag with thongs of leather.

'Has anyone told you what happened to the Three Strains after the passing of the Tuatha de Danann?' he asked.

I shook my head.

'When the Tuatha retreated into the burial mounds and became the faerie people, that we call the *sidhe*, they took the power of the Three Strains with them. It was an enchanted music and was rarely heard by mortals, though the *sidhe* would sometimes use it to lure a mortal to their land.'

The fili stood up, brushing the bracken from his robe.

'It is from the *sidhe* that we have the Noble Strains, he said, for some of us made it our task to listen and remember their music. And though we may have weakened it with our playing, yet it still contains their magic.'

'So after this,' he said, looking down at me with his fierce eyes, 'I hope that you will take more care of the emotions that you wake in others when you play your music. And perhaps, too, you will take more care of your harp. For, although it may not be as costly as the harps of the Sons of Uaithne, remember that it, too, has magic powers bound within it!'

Then he turned and strode down towards the village, his staff in his hand and his cloak flying out behind him.

4
The Birth of Cuchulainn

Druach held up his staff and his eyes burned in the light from the fire.

'Heroes', he bellowed, 'are born of gods and mortals. And the great Cuchulainn, warrior of Ulster, was no exception!'

He shook his silver branch, its shimmering music alerting us to the magic of a new tale.

'There are many stories of his birth,' he said, 'and many births of his within the stories!'

He threw back his head and laughed.

'But that is not so strange when you understand its meaning.'

Then he played a rousing tune and began his tale.

One day King Conchobor of Ulster was holding court at his palace at Emain Macha surrounded by all his noblemen. Although it was midday, they were feasting and laughing and enjoying the entertainment of bards and musicians, when suddenly the air became dark and a loud rushing sound like wind came to their ears. They ran out at once and saw a great flock of birds descending on the green beside the palace. The birds covered the plain like a sea of black waves and when they rose up again, they left it completely bald, stripped of grass even to the roots.

The warriors immediately called for their chariots to be harnessed and, leaping into them and lashing the horses, they went charging after the birds. Conchobar rode in the first chariot driven by his sister Dechtire, Fergus mac Roth the fiery chief of the Red Branch rode in the second, while close behind were Conall the Victorious and Bricriu the Poison-tongued, together with many other angry warriors.

Their song filling the air like perfume, the cloud of birds streaked ahead of them. They flew in nine groups, yoked together in pairs by silver chains that flashed in the pale sun. They led the warriors southwards across the mountain country of Slieve Fuait, across the Ford of Lethan and over the wide plain of Breg. As they neared the banks of the mysterious River Boyne, three birds detached themselves and flew on ahead of the rest. Soon afterwards dusk fell and the bird-cloak was swallowed up in the night sky.

As the men unharnessed their chariots, a whirl of snow blew round them. They set their horses loose to graze while Conall and Bricriu went in search of lodgings. The two men strode along the bank of the Boyne in the snow-flecked darkness hearing only the strange spell-like muttering of the restless river. They had not gone far when they saw before them the shadowy outline of the great burial mound of the Brugh, lying like a silent black drum beside the water. It seemed as if waves of power were coming from it, humming towards them through the air. And then they remembered that its time was very near, the time when the spear of Lugh the sun god would streak through its open portal and strike into its deep chamber.

Instinctively the two men turned round and began retracing their steps. As they did so, they caught sight of a small house lit by flickering firelight. They went towards it and a tall man and a beautiful woman came out to greet them. Hearing that the king needed shelter, they insisted that the whole company lodge at their house. But when the warriors arrived, the place was so small that they had to cram their chariots into the courtyard and jostle together inside the house. Nevertheless the storehouse was well stocked, and as soon as the men had eaten and drunk their fill, they lay down on the floor and fell into an exhausted sleep.

But in the heart of the night they were woken by a great cry. It came from the woman of the house whose time of childbirth had come upon her. Dechtire sprang up and went to help her. The woman's labour was swift and, just as the first streak of dawn appeared, and the spear of the sun god struck into the black chamber of the Brugh, the child was born. At the same instant a neighing cry came from outside the house and a mare gave birth to two foals.

When the commotion had died down, the warriors returned to sleep. But when they finally awoke, they found to their amazement that everything had disappeared – the man, his wife, the house and the animals. Nothing remained except the newborn child and the two newborn foals. The bemused Ulstermen took the boy and the foals back to the palace at Emain, where Conchobar gave the child to his sister Dechtire to foster.'

'And that was the first birth,' said Bruach softly, 'and, since it was in the time of snow and beside the Brugh, when else could it have been but Solstice night!'

He began rippling the harp strings with his fingers while he continued:

'But when the child reached boyhood, a sickness overtook him and he died. For three days Dechtire wandered the hills and fields weeping, taking neither food nor drink. But on the fourth she returned to the palace and called for a cup of water. A goblet was brought to her and as she tipped it towards her lips, a tiny creature slipped into her mouth. That night she dreamed a god appeared to her. His eyes were fiery stars, his hair blazed on his head and in his hand he held a flame-dripping spear. 'My name is Lugh,' he said, 'and it was by my will you travelled to the Brugh, the magic portal of the gods. The boy you birthed there was mine. I now plant him in your womb for second birthing. His name is Setanta. Raise him well.'

Soon afterwards, Dechtire found she was pregnant and was ashamed, not knowing how to speak about the dream. The king decided to marry her to the nobleman Sualdam, to cover her disgrace. But, before she came to the bridal bed, she brought a sickness on herself and cast out the child, making herself virgin again.'

The fili paused again.

'And that was the second birth. As to the third and final birth, that happened soon enough once Dechtire was wed, for within the year she was delivered of a boy child. And all took him to be Sualdam's son. But Dechtire called him Setanta.'

'And that', said the druid, wrapping his cloak around his shoulders, 'is how Cuchulainn received both a mortal and an immortal father. And how the child of the sun god was born at the dawning of the year.'

5

Lugh of the Shining Face

Next morning, Bruach found me again in the woods. I was listening to bird song.

'Everything speaks to you,' said the fili. 'if you have ears to listen.'

He sat down beside me.

'What do you know about Lugh?' he asked.

'I know he was Cuchulainn's father and that his fiery spear is one of the four sacred gifts of the Tuatha,' I replied.

'Good,' said Bruach. 'But do you know what his name means – for in it is his essence.'

'Light,' I said.

As soon as I had spoken the word, Bruach began to sing an incantation, spinning notes like sun-gold from his harp:

Lugh of shining face, and flowing golden hair,
Great god whose Long Arm flames across the sky.
Lugh the inspirer, radiant, luminous,
whose fiery spear flies burning to its mark.
Lugh Ildanach, the all-gifted One
who raises harvest riches from the earth.
Lugh the great sun lord, wielding power and might,
filled with bright knowledge, chief of all the gods. ⑥

When he had finished singing, he put down his harp.

When he was a child, Lugh was fostered by Manannan mac Lir, in the Land of Promise. There the boy enjoyed wonders without name, but most of all he loved to ride Aonbarr, the sea god's magic horse, which could carry him across land or sea. He especially loved riding it over the tips of the waves, where they were joined by a host of other white-maned horses that plunged across the billows with them. Lugh had a golden childhood in that land, but as soon as he reached manhood, he told Manannan he must return to Erin and free it from the Fomorian giants. Manannan gave Lugh his blessing and sent him out in his magic ship, the Ocean-Sweeper, laden with gifts.

The Ocean-Sweeper needed no oar or sail, for it was steered by thought alone. With the sea god's amber helmet haloing his head and his breastplate blazing with the sun's rays, Lugh stood up on the wooden boards and held aloft his magic sword, the Answerer. He stretched out his long arm until the great sword became a shaft of white light, running from hilt to tip. With it he reached across the sea and touched the land of Erin. Then he followed the shaft of light and came swiftly to the shore. Leaping out he sent the Ocean-Sweeper back across the sea and set out for the fortress of Nuada, king of the Tuatha.

The king was holding a great counsel of the nobles and gods of the Tuatha. All had assembled and the Gate Keeper was guarding the entrance of the palace when Lugh strode up with his shining face and asked to be let in. The Gate Keeper said sourly:

'Only those who can offer a skill can enter. What is your skill?'

'I am a smith,' replied Lugh.

'We already have a smith,' said the Gate Keeper.

'I am a warrior.'

'We have many of those,' said the Gate Keeper.

'I am a cupbearer and a harper.'

'We have both harpers and cupbearers in our company.'

'I am a physician.'

'We already have a physician.'

'I am a druid.'

'We have a druid.'

'That may be,' said Lugh, 'but is there a man among your company who possesses all these skills?'

The Gate Keeper shrugged and went into the palace to ask Nuada whether there was anyone at court who could boast of so many talents. The king was intrigued. 'Such a thing would be rare indeed,' he said. 'Let him come in and we shall test him.'

As soon as Lugh was admitted, he strode down the Great Hall and sat in the Sage's Seat. One by one, the gods and nobles began to test him, and soon found that he spoke the truth, for he was indeed adept in smithcraft, healing and all the other gifts of which he boasted.

But when dusk descended, there were two skills yet untested – the powers of might and music. So the great god Ogma decided to challenge his strength. There was a huge flagstone in the middle of the hall so heavy that it required a team of oxen to move it. Ogma heaved it up and hurled it out of the hall and into the courtyard. Lugh followed it outside, and a trail of fire streamed after him. He put his hands to the stone and sparks flew up his arms from his blazing fingers. He lifted the stone as lightly as if it were a mattress of feathers, and tossed it back into the centre of the hall. Then he strode back down the hall and demanded the Dagda's harp. The men told him that no one but the Dagda could play it. But as soon as he touched the harp the Three Noble Strains sprang to its strings. While he played, it seemed to the gods that the faces of the seasons passed before them, summoned by the power of each strain. When he finished, all agreed that in his hands the magic harp rang as powerfully as in those of his father.

'And that is how he became known as the Ildanach, the many-skilled,' said Bruach. 'And afterwards, recognizing his power, Nuada of the Silver Hand yielded him the kingship.' He paused. 'But you could say that it was the power of moon giving place to the power of sun.'

He stood up and tightened the girdle round his tunic.

'Tomorrow you shall hear more about his son Cuchulainn, a solar hero if ever there was one, and the inheritor of his father's skills and strengths. And watch out for the strange shining child who appears when he undergoes his tests. Who else could it be but his father come in disguise to give him a helping hand – and with a burning wheel at that!'

Laughing, he wrapped his cloak around him and strode off into the woods.

6
How Cuchulainn came by his Name

Next morning, after we had assembled again on the green, Bruach held up his staff, calling for our attention.

'The birth of a hero,' he said, 'is but the beginning. For even if he is half immortal and conceived of a god, he must still prove himself.'

He looked round at the crowd, his eyes shining. 'And how must he prove himself?' he asked.

When no one answered, he said:

'By tests of course! Tests of skill, tests of bravery, tests of prowess! And through one of these tests – and usually an early one at that, the hero discovers his real name and, with it, his true nature.'

The fili dropped his voice but his eyes still glittered.

'For those of us who undertake such tests, be they bard or warrior, the risks are great – for wild creatures lurk nearby, waiting to trap or help us. If we fail, they devour us, but if we succeed, they lend us their powers.'

As he said these words I felt a shiver of fear run up my spine. I had heard of the druid art of shape-shifting. I knew that druids had it, but I did not know the hero had this power too. Or perhaps it was different for him. Perhaps the druid took the creature's secret knowledge and the hero took its strength.

As I pondered all this, Bruach was already striking bold chords on his harp.

'For the first few years of his life,' he said, 'the boy was brought up by his mother at her home on Murtheimne Plain in the south east of Ulster. He listened to the tales of the Red Branch warriors at his uncle's court and his mind became filled with their glorious adventures. He longed to grow up quickly so that he could become one of them. And, indeed, he grew at a prodigious rate, as heroes do, and soon he became restless to visit the palace at Emain Macha and begin his training.'

He began to play a rhythmic melody.

'There is a story that he left his home at the age of five and set out on his own for the court, which meant crossing the Fuait Mountains. When he arrived at the palace he saw the famous boy troop playing on the green. He was so excited that he rushed in among them and tried to join in the game. Immediately they threw their javelins at him, but he parried them all with his little wooden shield. Then he set about him, dealing the boys strong blows with his fists.'

Bruach slapped his thigh and laughed.

'Of course, the king sent him back home to his mother. But the boys never stopped talking about him and so, a year later, he was called back to court to begin his proper training. This time, the boys greeted him with respect and he became their leader. And it was not long afterwards that he earned a new name - which is the story I will tell you now.'

The fili set his harp aside and, fixing us with his forceful gaze, began:

Now in the evenings, when they had finished their training for the day, Setanta and the boy troop used to play the game of Hurley together. This, to them, was a glorious battle. As soon as they faced each other in two lines upon the green, they became the Red Branch heroes. First they lifted up their hurley sticks, which immediately became their magic swords of light, and hailed each other. Then they raised their javelins. As each boy hurled his weapon, it seemed to him as though the fiery spear of Lugh shot flaming from his hand. Each spear streaked through the enemy and met its deadly mark. After that the boy troop made their charge. They ran among their foes, and caught their balls and hurled them back, and then let loose another hail of spears. Thus the fledgling warriors played their games each night and dreamed of future glory.

Now one day, King Conchobar came to take Setanta to a feast, but the boy, being immersed in his hurling combat with the boy troop asked if he might come on later when their game was ended. The king agreed and told him to follow on as soon as he was ready.

The game went on into the evening and dusk was already gathering as Setanta set out for the house of Culann the blacksmith, where the feast was being held. But he was so late in coming that the king and his retinue, who had already been at the house for some time, had forgotten about him. In fact, when Culann asked if any were still expected, Conchobar told him that they had all arrived.

'In that case,' said the smith, 'I will let my dog loose, for he guards my house and herds with his life. He is so ferocious that he would kill anyone who dared come near.'

Not long after the dog was let loose, Setanta approached

Culann's house. He could see the light shining from the windows of the hall and the shadowy outlines of the king and his men as they feasted. But as he began to cross the green he heard a low growl and a huge black shape slunk towards him, saliva dripping from its fangs.

The boy fingered his toy weapons, the little hurley stick and the ball, and faced the hound. As the hairs rose on the back of the crouching animal, so the hairs on the boy's head stood up. As the hound's eyes rolled, one of the boy's eyes shrank into his head, while the other bulged forward. As the hound bared its teeth, the boy's lips peeled back and his teeth stretched across his face from ear to ear. As the hound pressed its back legs towards the earth and prepared to spring, the muscles of the boy's calves and thighs spun round and tightened. As the hound leaped upon him, its great jaws gaping, the boy raised his own ferocious face, and with a roar that matched the roaring of the beast itself, thrust his hurley ball with all his might down the creature's throat. The ball shot through the hound's body and drove out its entrails. Then the boy heaved up its carcass and flung it against a pillar of the house, crushing its head.

As soon as the men inside heard the yell of the hound, they suddenly remembered that Setanta was coming alone to the house. They rushed out in horror expecting to find the boy dead, but saw him instead standing triumphantly astride the body of the hound, still half-transformed by the warp-spasm that had come upon him. Overwhelmed with amazement and relief, Fergus mac Roth lifted the boy up and paraded him on his shoulders. He carried him into the feasting hall where he was given a hero's welcome. After that the wine flowed freely in celebration. Only

Culann kept from joining in the merriment, for he was grieving for his faithful hound.

As soon as he saw Culann's sadness, Setanta ran up to him.

'Don't worry,' he said, 'I will train a pup to guard your house just as well as the one I killed. And meanwhile, I will guard the house for you myself!'

This offer was greeted with roars of approval from the assembled company. There and then they named the boy Cuchulainn, the Hound of Culann. He was only six years old when he earned this name, and he was known by it all his life.

Bruach played a last flourish on his harp and looked round at us. He said: 'And that is how by meeting the ferocity of a beast, and afterwards taking on its role, Cuchulainn discovered his name and nature. Later, of course, he would become the guard dog for the whole of Ulster. But that, as they say, is another story!'

Then he gave us one of his rare smiles and walked off towards his hut.

7
Cuchulainn's Wooing of Emer

After we had eaten, we gathered again on the green and waited for Bruach. Soon we saw his wild figure coming out of his hut and walking towards us. I thought he had a more jaunty air about him and I was right, for his eyes were less fierce than usual and even showed a flash of merriment as he looked at us.

As if we needed proof of his mood, the fili played us a jig on the harp and when he had finished said:

Now, remember we left our hero in the middle of his youthful training. Well, he soon grew into a young man, so good-looking that he quickly became the darling of the women at court. Even so, he was not so swift at proving his prowess in the arts of love as he was in the arts of combat.

In the opinion of the men of Ulster, however, Cuchulainn had three defects, which were that he was too young – for his beard was not yet grown, he was too daring for his own good and he was too handsome for their liking. Soon they began to mutter together that it was time he found himself a wife. Hearing their comments, Cuchulainn decided to woo a woman that he had seen in the Gardens of Lugh. She was Emer, daughter of Forgall, famed for her beauty and her wisdom.

Before setting out, Cuchulainn dressed himself in his finest clothing. Next to his skin he wore a white shirt intricately embroidered with gold thread, over it he wore a dark red tunic heavily folded and fastened with a large gold brooch. The gilded hilt of a sword gleamed at his side and a crimson shield rimmed with silver and engraved with gold figures of birds and animals, hung from his shoulders.

Cuchulainn's chariot was almost as magnificent as the man himself. It was made of wood and wicker with wheels of white bronze. It had a high copper frame and a yoke of gold to hold the horses. The two horses that drove the chariot were the Grey of Macha and the Black of Saingliu, the two foals that had been born on the same day as Cuchulainn himself. These fiery animals snorted and tossed their heads as Cuchulainn climbed into his seat. His charioteer, Laeg, sprang up and stood in front of him. Slender as a willow, with a bronze band around his head and a fine gold net holding back his long curls, he swept his cloak aside to free his bare arms, took up the plaited yellow reins and raised his red gold whip.

It was said in Ulster that there was no chariot to touch that of Cuchulainn when Laeg was driving it. The forces of the four elements themselves propelled it. The high-sided copper frame streaked through the landscape like a fiery coin. Dust whipped from the hooves of the sleek-muscled horses and their manes flowed like waves between the fields.

Cuchulainn arrived at the Gardens of Lugh in a whirl of gold and clanking weapons. Emer was sitting on the green, teaching needlework to her foster-sisters. She looked up at the loud noise but could not tell what it was that went flying past them. She asked one of the women to go and see. Her sister Fial went across to the edge of the green and immediately came running back saying:

'It's a fine chariot driven by two horses, a black and a grey, and seated in it is a man magnificently dressed.'

But even as she spoke Cuchulainn had dismounted and was making his way towards Emer.

'May the blessings of the gods attend you!' he said.

Emer looked up at him, her needlework across her lap:

'And may they smooth your path,' she replied.

'May the apple of your eye perceive wisdom,' he said.

'Where have you come from?' she asked.

'From Intide Emna.'

She looked down at her embroidered work.

'Where did you sleep?'

'At the house of a cattle-herder on the plain of Tethra,' he said, noticing that the thick curls of her hair were caught back by a copper pin.

'What food were you served?'

'Oh,' he said, 'some ruin of a chariot!'

She laughed at this and her two white breasts trembled in the neck of her gown.

He bent towards her.

'We came,' he said, 'between the two Mountains of the Wood.'

She stood up quickly and the blood rose in her cheeks.

'Which way did you go after that?'

Cuchulainn replied in the dark speech: 'That is not hard. From the cave of the sea, through the Great Secret of the Tuatha de Danann, from the foaming breath of the two great horses of

Macha, over the garden of the Morrigan, over the back of the Great Sow, between the god and the seer, between the boar and his dam, over the Washing-pool of the horses of Dea, between the king and his servant, to the king of the Four Corners of the World, between the Great Vat and the Little Vat, to the Gardens of Lugh, and to the daughters of Forgall, the Fomorian king.'

His eyes bored into hers. 'And what about you?'

'That, too, is not hard,' she said, answering him in the riddling tongue: 'I am Tara, the queen of women, purest white of maidens, a beacon of chastity, a goblet undrunk, a seer that observes but does not see. A woman forbidden, a dragon untouched. A king's daughter, a fire of hospitality, a path untrodden.'

She added in plain speech: 'But I am guarded by champions so that I may never be carried off against their will and without my father's consent.'

'My strength is equal to thirty men and I can fight alone against forty.' said Cuchulainn.

'That is impressive for one so young and tender,' said Emer smiling.

Cuchulainn looked at her breasts lying inside her dress.

'In that fair land I'll rest my weapon!' he said.

'No one can come to that land,' said Emer, 'unless he has killed a hundred men at every ford from the Ford of Scennmen to the Ford of Banchuing.'

Cuchulainn said again: 'In that fair land I'll rest my weapon.'

'No one can come to that land,' she replied, 'unless he has leaped three walls with a salmon's leap and killed three groups of nine men at a blow, leaving the middle man standing. And after that brought from the stronghold of King Forgall, my own weight in gold.'

'In that fair land I'll rest my weapon,' said Cuchulainn.

'No one may come to this land who has not gone without sleep from Samain, at the Summer's rest, to Imbolc, when Brigid's lambs cry for their milk, and from Beltain, when the maiden rises, to the feast of Lugh and the time of earth's sleeping.'

'As you command, so is it done,' said Cuchulainn.

Then Cuchulainn returned to his chariot and drove back to Emain. Meanwhile the women went inside and told everyone in the court about the coming of the warrior from Ulster. They said that he and Emer had spoken the dark speech with each other and that they had not been able to understand it. When this report reached the ears of Emer's father, Forgall, he exclaimed: 'So the madman of Emain Macha has come here and spoken to Emer, has he! Well if she has fallen in love with him it will do her no good, for I shall put an end to it!'

Bruach pushed his cloak aside and stood up. He said:

And so the wily father went to Emain Macha in disguise and suggested that Cuchulainn should go for training to Scathach, the famous warrior woman of Alba. He did this to try and lure Cuchulainn to his death, for Scathach was so ferocious that few could undergo her training and remain alive. But, unable to resist such a challenge, Cuchulainn swore before the entire assembly that he would go to Scathach and receive her training.

8
Cuchulainn's Training in Arms

Next day, after we had gathered again, Bruach surveyed the crowd and when his eyes met mine, gave me a knowing look.

'Now, in the understanding of a fili, the tests of a hero come from the four great pillars of the universe,' he said. 'Is there anyone here who can tell me what they are?'

His eyes surveyed the gathering crowd expectantly. When no one replied, he looked at me enquiringly.

'The four great forces of nature – earth, fire, air and water.' I replied at once.

'Good,' said Bruach, 'the four great forces indeed. For, without their joint powers, the world would lose its balance and all would become chaos.'

He bent over his harp and struck a cluster of chords and notes from the middle of the strings, using his nails and finger-ends by turns, so that the music seemed to jump and spark out of the instrument.

'The first test,' he said, above the din, 'was the Test by Fire.'

He dropped his voice and, as the sounds echoed away he said:

It was in Alba at the house of the warrior Domnall that Cuchulainn learned his first great feat and for it he had to dance upon a heated flagstone until his feet became as light and lithe as the flickering flames themselves. As he practised it the soles of his feet turned hard and black. This test was known as the Feat of the Pierced Flagstone. But, to the druid's understanding, it was the Test by Fire.

Bruach bent over his harp and raised from it again the fiery sounds we heard before. He played for a short while, then he said:

After he had mastered this feat, Cuchulainn continued on his journey east across Alba. And this is how he came upon his second test, the Test by Earth.

As he approached Scathach's stronghold his way was barred by a strange dark plain, known as the Plain of Ill-luck. It bound the feet of all who tried to cross and cut them with its sharp blades. Cuchulainn stopped a youth with shining hair who he saw standing nearby and asked him how he could cross the plain. The youth gave him a wheel and told him to roll it across the plain and follow its tracks. Cuchulainn took his advice and when he rolled the wheel it gave out sparks of heat that burned a safe path through the bog. Thus, by the power of fire, he crossed to the other side and passed the Test of Earth.

As he spoke these words, the fili drew strong chords from the low strings in his harp and the deep sounds reverberated round the clearing, holding us with their strength and firmness.

'But the Test by Air was yet to come,' said Bruach, straightening up.

For, beyond the Plain of Ill-luck, lay the Perilous Glen. The luminous boy had warned him that on this road, which lay between the overhanging slopes of mountains, he would find himself attacked by wild animals. Cuchulainn set out along the road and was soon enveloped in mist. Then it seemed that visions rose before him, fierce creatures loomed up and leaped upon him, while sharp-taloned eagles darted at his eyes. He warded them off with blows, but it was not his blows that overcame them so much as his courage and defiance. Then a great hag flew at him on the wind, screeching like a bird of prey. He aimed a blow at her head and at once she wheeled away, flapping and squawking. With growing anger Cuchulainn whirled his sword about him, hacking at the fearful creatures until at last the mist cleared and the startling images and visions that it carried whirled down the mountainside and disappeared into the valley below. Thus, because he trusted the powers of earth and stood his ground against the visions, Cuchulainn also passed the Test by Air.

As he spoke Bruach reached for his harp again and began to run his finger-ends across the strings so that they whistled and sighed and sang like the wind blowing across the plain.

And now as to the Test by Water, this was the fourth and last test that waited for Cuchulainn. When at last he came in sight of Scathach's island, he saw that he had to cross a bridge to reach it. The bridge was high and narrow and passed over a deep gorge full of churning water. As he came near, Cuchulainn saw a company of warriors on the green. He discovered that they were training with Scathach and asked them why they were not on the island. One of them replied: 'None of us has been able to get across because as soon as we put any weight on it, the bridge tips up and pitches us on the ground. It needs a special leap to cross it, which is the last feat that Scathach teaches us. Until then we are prevented from reaching the island.'

Hearing this, Cuchulainn ran at the bridge and made a high leap into the air, but he landed short and was thrown back on the bank. Three times he tried to cross the bridge and three times he failed. Then, with the jeers of the students ringing in his ears, he began to transform into his famous warp-spasm. The hairs of his head stood up on end and flamed like the rays of the sun itself, the muscles of his calves and thighs revolved back to front, his mouth peeled open to the width of his face, while one eye sank deep into his face and the other bulged outwards, staring with a mad fury. In this aspect Cuchulainn ran again at the bridge and performed his Hero's Salmon-leap, which carried him to the middle of it. Then the bridge tipped forward and threw him onto Scathach's island.

Thus it was that, by means of the power of air, Cuchulainn leaped over the treacherous gorge and passed the Test by Water.

As he spoke Bruach began working his fingers lightly and fast over the upper harp-strings until it seemed as if the whole green and even the hills themselves were filled with the sound of silvery rippling. On and on he played until our heads and ears were rinsed and ringing with it. As the echoes died away he said:

Three days later, when Scathach was sitting on the green in front of a yew-tree, Cuchulainn again made his great Salmon-leap and landed in front of her. Before she could move, he had drawn his sword and placed it between her breasts.

'I will take your life,' he said, 'unless you grant me three things!'

Scathach turned her battle-scarred face towards him and regarded him coolly.

'If you can name them in one breath they are yours,' she said.

'I desire you to train me in arms, to give me your daughter for my bed and to make a prophecy concerning me.'

Scathach agreed to his requests and he stayed with her until he had mastered all the feats of battle and all the skills she had to teach him.

'And if you want to know,' said the fili, stealing a glance at us, 'these were the feats!'
Then he began to play a jig faster and faster, at the same time bellowing out their names:

The apple-feat, the thunder-feat, the blade-feat, the feat of the shield-rim, the supine-feat, the javelin-feat, the rope-feat, the body-feat, the cat's-feat, the pole-throw, the crouch of a chariot-chief, the wheel-feat, the breath-feat, the hero's cry, the stunning blow, the counter-blow, the feat of the lance-point, the feat of the scythe-chariot, the twisting of the hero on spear points and, the most deadly feat of all, the *gae bolga*!

Bruach ended the jig with a resounding chord and put his harp down. His face becoming serious again, he said:

When he had learned all these, Scathach prepared her prophecy, calling on the gods to send her inspiration in a vision-dream. After she had dreamed, she came to Cuchulainn and spoke these words to him:

Cuchulainn of the Victories,
battle-hard warrior of the Cattle Raid,
great peril is your fate. I see you stand
alone against a host. One man
against a mighty warrior crowd –
your prowess tested to the uttermost.
Blood and slaughter are your destiny,
strength of might alone sustains you.
Mighty hero, victor of a thousand battles,
brave defender of beloved Ulster,
short will be your life, a burst of glory.
But afterwards your flame
will burn forever. ⑦⑧

When she had delivered this prophecy Cuchulainn took his leave of Scathach, who had taught him all the arts of war, and kissed her daughter, Uathach, from whom he had learned all the arts of love.

'And there are those,' said the fili eyeing the women in the crowd, 'who consider both arts require an equal training!'

So saying, with a last melodious flourish, he put his harp aside and left us to our thoughts.

9
The Pillow-talk

'In case you are not aware of it,' said Bruach, looking at us quizzically, 'let me tell you that women rule the land! In fact, not only do they rule it, they *are* the land.'

He looked round at the men.

'If you cannot see it for yourself, let me remind you that our Mother Earth is the Great Goddess herself. The smooth, rolling hills are her breasts, the mountain-slopes her reclining limbs, the trees her flowing tresses and the valleys her dark and secret places.'

Holding up his staff, in a loud voice he declared: 'Listen and understand this mystery! In the Goddess' hand is the gift of Sovereignty, a gift which the king must win from her, for he is her chosen consort.'

He pulled his harp towards him and began fingering the strings.

'In the stories of Erin,' he said, 'there are many great queens whose names still strike terror into the hearts of men and whose courage and daring rivals the bravest heroes. Such a queen was Medbh.

Striking a chord on his harp, he sang this invocation:

> Great Sovereign Medbh,
> Intoxicating One,
> the strength of ten brave warriors
> rests within your arm.

Undaunted, battle-eager, wielding royal power,
strong men quail before you, armies fear your wrath,
in fear the rivers run from you,
the fields lie trembling as you pass.
Unconquered, wild, majestic, all Connaght
you command. In your realm you reign supreme,
Peerless champion and alluring queen. ⑨

Bruach put his harp aside and lifted up his silver branch, shaking it to announce his story. Then he began:

Medbh was queen of Connacht and ruled from her palace at Cruachan. Her palace was huge and imposing. It was built out of oak and had sixteen glass windows flanked with shutters of bronze. Inside were seven great halls, each one containing couches for the queen and all her warriors. The walls of each hall were lined with wooden panels carved with elaborate designs, and in the centre of the palace was a raised dais encased in silver, surrounded by four blazing bronze pillars that supported the roof. On this dais Medbh had her great throne and it was here that she sat in state, her heavy purple cloak folded about her, and her two gold birds perched on her shoulders. Whenever she wished to summon her courtiers, she would strike one of the great bronze pillars with her silver wand.

One morning when Medbh, queen of Connacht and her husband Ailill were lying together in the great royal bed, Ailill made a rash remark. He turned his head on the pillow and said to Medbh:

'It is good for a woman to be married to a wealthy husband.'

'It is indeed,' said the queen, ' but what made you say that?'

'Because I was just thinking how much better off you are today than you were the day I married you,' said Ailill.

'I was as well off as this before I ever met you!' Medbh retorted.

'Is that so?' said Ailill, 'I thought you only had the woman's things you brought with you.'

'On the contrary, my father gave me the whole province of Cruachan!'

She raised herself on her elbow and her eyes blazed.

'And at one time I had suitors from all over Erin seeking my hand and offering me wealth and lands. Men from Leinster, Tara and Ulster, warriors, captains and kings, all came here asking to marry me. I could have had any of them, except the bride-price I required was such a hard one, harder than any of them could provide.'

She glanced at Ailill.

'And you know perfectly well what that was. Instead of a man with gifts, I wanted a husband who was *lacking* in three qualities – namely greed, fear and jealousy!'

She climbed out of bed and put on a robe of crimson silk trimmed with white fur.

'And as to why he should lack the first of these,' she thundered, 'it is because I am so generous that it would be a disgrace to be married to a man who refused to give gifts and bounty to his people. As to the second, I am so bold in battle and so lively in combat that to have a timid husband would be unthinkable. As to the third, it is common knowledge that I have never yet enjoyed a man without there being another waiting in his shadow.' She tossed her head. 'So that to have a jealous husband would be an impossibility! And I chose you, Ailill, as my husband, for the lack of these qualities and not for your wealth or possessions. In fact, if you remember, it was *I* who gave *you* a bride-price. I brought you armour for twelve warriors, a costly chariot, a plate of gold as big as your face, and a bar of bronze as big as your arm. So, in regard to wealth, it is you who are a kept man, for my fortune is much greater than yours!'

Ailill replied indignantly: 'You can hardly call me a kept man. I may not be as rich as my two older brothers, but I have always been your equal!'

Medbh laughed.

'I hardly think so,' she said, 'considering my fortune is greater than yours!'

'How can you say so?' retorted Ailill. 'When you know perfectly well that I have more wealth and property than anyone!'

The quarrel raged between them for days until at last they decided to make a tally of their possessions to find out which of them was the wealthiest. So they commanded their servants to bring out their possessions one by one and count them. Their humblest pots and pails were counted, then their cauldrons and jugs, their clothes and shoes and jewellery. Then they made their servants bring in their herds and number the heads of sheep and cattle, and after that to bring their horses from the paddocks and count them, and also to count their goats, pigs, rams and boars, and every last thing that each of them possessed. And when all had been counted, they found that their properties were equally matched, with one exception. Ailill owned Finnbennach the White-horned, a rare and magical bull that had once been among Medbh's herds, but had left to join the herd of Ailill. And now

Medbh had no bull its equal.

Medbh was angry when she discovered this. It seemed to her that unless she owned property equal to her husband's, then she might as well own none at all. She summoned her steward Mac Roth, and asked him if there was a bull in the whole of Erin that could rival Finnbennach the White-horned. Mac Roth said that he only knew of one, the Brown Bull of Cuailnge, which was owned by Daire of Ulster. So Medbh sent Mac Roth to ask Daire to loan her the Brown Bull for a year.

'Tell Daire,' she said, 'that at the year's end I will return the bull together with fifty heifers, and also tell him that if that is not enough, I will give him a portion of land, a magnificent chariot and, on top of that, the favours of my own thighs!'

So Mac Roth travelled to Ulster taking with him nine of Medbh's attendants. When they arrived at Daire's house they were given a great welcome and as they feasted Daire asked Mac Roth what had brought him to Ulster. Mac Roth told him about the quarrel between Medbh and Ailill and why Medbh wanted the Brown Bull. When he told him the terms Medbh was offering, Daire leaped up and down on his feather couch with such force that he split its seams.

'By the gods!' he exclaimed, 'whatever the people of Ulster say, Medbh can certainly borrow this treasure. The Brown will be delivered to the land of Connacht without delay. You have my word on it!'

Mac Roth was delighted with this answer. In celebration, he and the other messengers drank a great quantity of wine that night. Afterwards in a state of drunkenness one of them said to the other:

'The man of this house is certainly good and generous.'

'That's true,' replied the other.

'I'd say there is no one among the people of Ulster better than he.'

'The only man better, is Conchobar, the king of Ulster,' said the other. Then he added: 'But it's as well that Daire has agreed to Medbh's terms, for otherwise she would have raised the forces of four provinces to take the bull from him.'

Daire's chief steward who was hovering nearby, overheard them speaking and became very angry. Next morning he went to Daire and said: 'Is it true that you have promised to lend the bull to Medbh?'

'Yes,' Daire replied.

'It was not for you to make such a promise. Now they are saying that if you had not agreed to give it, they would have taken the bull by force.'

As soon as he heard this Daire summoned Mac Roth and told him that he had decided not to let him take the bull. The steward was astonished and asked what had made him change his mind so suddenly. When Daire told him about the conversation, Mac Roth pleaded with him not to put such weight on the words of drunken servants.

'Nevertheless,' said Daire, 'Medbh shall not have the bull if I can help it.'

Unable to persuade Daire to change his mind, the messengers were forced to return to Cruachan empty handed. But when Mac Roth told Medbh what had happened, she said: 'Surely it was common knowledge that if Daire would not let me have the Brown Bull, I would take it from him by force.'

'And,' she added, looking at him fiercely, 'take it I will!' Bruach paused and looked at us. His eyes were dark.

'Thus began the great battle between Connacht and Ulster', he said, 'which was afterwards known as the *Tain Bo Cuailnge*, the Cattle-Raid of Cooley. It was the battle in which Cuchulainn won his glory, but not without great cost, as you shall hear tomorrow.'

10

Cuchulainn and Edarcomhol

The fili shook his golden branch and some who were still far off hurried to the green to hear him.

'Today I have a story for you that you may think is rather silly,' he said. 'But in it you will see the struggle our great hero had between his war-like impulses and his feeling for Fergus mac Roth, his foster father.'

He kept speaking while he uncovered his harp.

'Like all the sons of kings and nobles, Cuchulainn was fostered as a child. In fact all the best men of the land had a share in his upbringing. But his greatest bond was with Fergus, chief of the Red Branch warriors. In this story you will see how much Cuchulainn respected and honoured him, even though – and for very good reasons, Fergus had by now defected to Medbh's army.

The fili gave a short laugh and, eyeing the men among us, added: 'Of course, Cuchulainn's admiration for Fergus was purely for his military prowess – though it is said that the man's sexual prowess was equally impressive!'

Then, playing a jaunty jig on his harp, he began:

Ailill and Medbh had a foster-son called Edarcomhol who was haughty and overbearing. He told Fergus that he wanted to meet Cuchulainn.

'I don't want you to go,' said Fergus.

'Why?' asked Edarcomhol.

'When I think of your arrogance and sarcasm and the recklessness and wild temper of Cuchulainn, I cannot see that any good will come of it,' said Fergus.

'Can't you get protection for me?' asked Edarcomhol.

'Only if you promise not to goad him,' said Fergus.

'I swear I will keep my tongue bridled and not ask him for combat until the day of doom itself,' said the other.

So the two men rode in their two chariots and came to where Cuchulainn was camped. Cuchulainn was playing a game of draughts with Laeg, his charioteer, and had his back towards the newcomers.

'I can see a chariot approaching,' said Laeg. 'In it is a huge yellow-haired man, as big as a tree. He has a purple cloak around him fringed with gold, he carries a curved red shield, and there is a sword as long as a currach's oar lying across his knees.'

'That is Fergus,' said Cuchulainn, 'and, for all its size, the scabbard across his knees is hollow. For I heard that when Ailill caught him sleeping with Medbh he took away his sword and replaced it with a wooden one!'

'And now I see another chariot coming with a young man sitting in it,' said Laeg, 'it's careering along at great speed drawn by two fine horses.'

'That will be one of the youths of Connacht come to have a look at me,' said Cuchulainn. 'Although I am famous in their camp, none of them have seen me.

At that moment Fergus drew level with Cuchulainn and jumped down from his chariot.

'Welcome father Fergus,' said Cuchulainn, 'if a fish is found in the river, may you have a salmon and a half, if a flock of birds alights on the plain, may you have a wild goose and a half!'

'I do believe you really mean such welcome!' said Fergus. The two men embraced. Then he gave Cuchulainn the message from Medbh saying that she agreed to let him meet her men in single combat.

Having delivered his message Fergus went away. But Edarcomhol remained and stood staring at Cuchulainn.

'What are you staring at?' asked the hero.

'You,' replied Edarcomhol.

'The eye has observed that,' said Cuchulainn.

'I cannot see why men speak of you with awe,' said the other. 'I see nothing fearful or terrible about you. Instead I see a pretty boy with toy weapons and a few slick tricks!'

Cuchulainn looked him up and down.

'In spite of your insolence, I will not kill you for Fergus' sake,' he said, 'otherwise be sure your entrails would by now be spread throughout the camp.'

'Don't you dare threaten me!' said the other, 'for you can be sure that when tomorrow comes, I shall be the first to come against you!'

'In that case I shall wait for you,' said Cuchulainn.

Edarcomhol went back to his chariot and was driving away when suddenly he said to his charioteer:

'I have just arranged to fight with Cuchulainn tomorrow, but now I can't wait that long. Turn round and we'll go and meet him.'

Laeg said to Cuchulainn: 'That chariot has turned round and is coming back again.'

The two men watched as it drove towards the ford.

'Edarcomhol is wanting me to fight him,' said Cuchulainn, 'but I shall have to refuse him because of the honour I owe my foster-father, Fergus.'

Then Cuchulainn went to the ford, and Edarcomhol demanded that they engage in single combat without delay.

'I am not interested,' said Cuchulainn.

'That's too bad.' replied Edarcomhol.

Then Cuchulainn cut a swathe in the ground beneath his feet so that the man fell over backwards and the clod of earth landed on his stomach.

'Go away,' he said, 'if it were not for the debt I owe Fergus you would by now have been cut into small pieces!'

But still Edarcomhol insisted on combat.

'We will not part from here until either I take your head or you take mine!' he said.

In answer Cuchulainn flicked his sword across the other's armpits so that his clothes fell to the ground but his skin remained untouched.

'Now go!' he said.

'No!' came the reply.

Then Cuchulainn trimmed the young man's hair with the blade of his sword, leaving his skin unscathed. But Edarcomhol continued to goad him.

Finally, Cuchulainn took his sword and passed it from the crown of the man's head down to the navel.

When Fergus saw Etarcomhol's empty chariot coming back, he asked his charioteer: 'Where is your lord?'

'He is lying dead at the ford, killed by Cuchulainn,' the man replied.

Fergus went to the ford and saw the body. He came back and turned on Cuchulainn in fury.

'You little devil!' he shouted, 'Why are you so perverse? That man had my protection!'

Cuchulainn threw himself on the ground in front of his foster-father, begging him not to be angry but Fergus ordered his chariot be driven over Cuchulainn three times. Afterwards Cuchulainn remonstrated with him, saying: 'Go and ask his charioteer who was to blame?'

'It was not Cuchulainn's fault,' said the charioteer.

'That's true, Father Fergus,' said Cuchulainn, 'he refused to leave without either my taking his head or he taking mine! Would you have liked him to have taken mine?'

After Fergus had heard the whole story he said: 'The insolent dog should not have meddled with so great a hound!'

He tied the man's heels together and attached him to the back of his chariot. Then he drove his chariot back to Medbh's camp.

11
Cuchulainn and the Morrigan

'If you understand the power of the Goddess,' said Bruach, 'you will know that she has both a fair and a dark face. It is dangerous to cross her, even when she shows her fair face. But the man who pits himself against the Dark Goddess, is rash indeed.

'The very name of the Morrigan should strike fear into our hearts, for it means the Phantom. The Morrigan is the goddess of war, the darkest and fiercest of our goddesses. Together with her bloodthirsty sisters, Badbh and Nemhain, she broods over the battlefield. She commands the powers of death and life, and often alights on those about to die in the form of her totem bird, the raven.'

Then he struck a deep metallic chord on his harp and as he began to sing it seemed as if the voice of the goddess herself rose rasping above him:

Great Morrigan, dark queen,
fierce web-winged warrior.
Crow-formed above the battle-field
with Badbh and Nemhain, your frenzied sisters
you soar and scream.
Destroyer Goddess, blood-dark, beautiful,
fire-haired, seductive challenger of gods.
Fearsome prophetess

and phantom Washer at the Ford.
Life-shadower, death-dealer,
brave men fear you; heroes bend
before your ancient wisdom,
fertile, fearful, sacrificial,
Cailleach,
Queen. ⑩

Bruach paused, while the flames of the fire rose up and the fear of her sent shivers through our hearts.

'But she has gifts to give us,' said the fili, 'gifts of power and daring, strength and wisdom, even gifts of prophecy if we dare to trust her. But a hero can be proud and scornful of women, and set too much store on his own strength. Instead of accepting the help of the goddess, he can reject and challenge her. So it was with Cuchulainn. And while we might admire his strength and courage, perhaps he was foolish to try to outwit her, for rejection angers her. But listen while I tell this story and then you may judge Cuchulainn's wisdom for yourselves.'

Bruach struck three great chords on his harp, which resonated round the clearing. Then he began:

One evening when Cuchulainn was resting outside his camp recovering from the day's fighting, he heard a loud clattering and saw a woman approaching in a high bronze carriage driven by a chestnut horse. She had long red hair bound with a circlet of gold, dark eyes beneath fiery red eyebrows while over her slim body she wore a silk dress that shone with many colours. A long heavy cloak was caught round her neck by a jewelled brooch. It fell in folds beside the wheels of her chariot and dragged on the ground. Her face was stiff as ivory and she held herself like a queen.

She rode up to Cuchulainn and stopped her chariot inches from his feet, where he lay on the ground. Too exhausted to rise he merely looked up at her.

'Who are you?' he asked.

'I am the daughter of King Buan,' she answered, 'and I have brought all my wealth and cattle to give to you.'

When he neither moved nor answered her, she said: 'I have conceived a great love for you because of the tales I have heard of your prowess.'

Cuchulainn raised himself on one arm and regarded his bloodstained battle shirt and leather breeches. He felt the weariness draining through his body.

'You have come to me at a bad time,' he said, 'I am not in full health. I am exhausted and short of food. I am unable to think of women at the moment.'

'Ah, but I might be able to help you,' said the woman, dismounting and pulling her cloak from the wheel spokes.

Cuchulainn regarded her with dull eyes.

'It was not for the backside of a woman that I took on this war!' he said and sank down into the grass.

The woman said in a new and imperious voice: 'If you refuse me I shall come against you.'

Cuchulainn turned his head and saw two fiery points on her cheeks and two red flames in her eyes as she stood over him.

'When you are fighting I shall come against you in the shape of an eel, wind myself round your ankles and trip you up in the ford!' she said.

'This is much easier to believe,' said Cuchulainn, raising himself from the ground, 'for I doubt you are the daughter of a king.'

He stood up and took a step towards her: 'If you come against me as an eel,' he said in a voice of low menace, ' I shall smash your eel's ribs with the toes of my foot, and you will carry that mark until I lift it from you.'

'Is that so?' she replied, spitting out her words like wood-sparks. 'Then I will come against you as a she-wolf and drive the wild beasts into the ford to harry you!'

Cuchulainn felt his hair rising up in points on his head, 'I shall aim a sling-stone at your eye so that it bursts inside your head. And you shall also carry that mark until I lift it from you.'

'If you dare do such a thing,' said the woman, her voice cold as a sword-blade, 'I will come at you as a hornless red heifer with a herd of red-eared cattle at my back and trample you in the ford!'

Cuchulainn began striding back towards the camp, struggling to contain the battle-frenzy that was rising in him. Without looking back he shouted: 'Then I will hurl a great stone at your leg and shatter it. And that is another mark that you will have forever unless I lift it from you with my blessing!'

He turned and lifted his arm, but as he did so, the woman sprang into her carriage, set the whip to her horse, and rode away, faster than the wind. As he watched, horse, carriage and woman were blotted out by a hail of clods and dried earth. Then he heard the loud rattle of a raven close by his ear.

A few days afterwards, Cuchulainn went out to meet the Connacht warrior Loch who had challenged him to single combat. The two men met at a ford and began making feats of swordplay and striking blows at each other. Cuchulainn was just beginning to get the upper hand when an eel slipped out of the water and knotted itself in three coils around his ankles. Cuchulainn fell back into the ford and Loch slashed at him so that his blood streamed into the water.

'Quick,' said one of the Ulstermen who were watching, 'urge him on, or he will die from disheartenment.'

As soon as he heard this, Bricriu, the poison-tongued, began to goad him.

'So much for your strength if a little salmon can bind you at a time like this!' he said jeeringly. 'What made you think you could take on a hero's task if this is the best you can do!'

Cuchulainn felt anger pulse through him. He roused himself and struck at the eel with the point of his foot, crushing its ribs.

With his feet released he again harried Loch with powerful sword-thrusts and blows. Then a she-wolf appeared and began chasing the cattle in the field. Cuchulainn aimed a slingshot at the wolf so that the stone entered its eye and was driven back into its head. After that a hornless red heifer appeared before the cattle and led them in a mad dash across the fords and pools, churning up the meadow all around. Then Cuchulainn heaved up a boulder from the water and threw it at the heifer's legs.

Cuchulainn attacked Loch again with his sword and called for Laeg, his charioteer, to make ready the *gae bolga* by sending it along the stream to him. He caught it and, positioning it in the fork of his foot, launched it at Loch. It pierced deep into his body and sprang out its barbs. Loch pitched forward onto the ground in front of Cuchulainn and Cuchulainn bent down and cut off his head with one stroke.

Afterwards he returned to the Ulster camp in great fatigue and sat down on the grass. As soon as he did so, an old squint-eyed woman came limping towards him leading a cow that had three teats. She stopped near him and began to milk the cow. Cuchulainn asked her to give him a drink. She pulled on the first teat until it was dry and gave him the milk.

'A blessing on you, old woman!' said Cuchulainn. The woman turned away her head as her eye became whole. Then she began pulling at the next teat. Cuchulainn begged her for a second drink. When she gave it to him, he said again:

'A blessing on you!'

She bent to the third teat and he asked again for a drink. When she gave that to him he blessed her a third time. Then the old woman straightened up, her body and legs now healed and whole.

'You swore you would never heal me!' she said to him in the barbed voice that he recognized.

Cuchulainn looked up and saw again the slim woman with the long red hair, the fiery eyebrows and the dark eyes.

'If I had known it was you, I would never have done it!' he said.

The fili stood up, his face glowing in the embers of the fire.

'But that was not the end of it,' he said, 'for afterwards she waited for him.' He pulled his cloak around him. 'Nor did she have long to wait. As you will see tomorrow.'

Then he swung his harp over his shoulder and went off into the night.

12
The Death of Cuchulainn

'And now,' said Bruach, after he had shaken his silver branch, 'I have a sad tale to tell. It is the death of Cuchulainn. But do not be too sad, for it was his chosen fate to die while still in his youthful strength and glory. In this story you will see how he begins to break his *geasa*, the magical taboos laid upon him in his life. For, just as mystical signs heralded his birth, so they also appear at his death – which, as you know, is just another gateway.'

He leaned towards his harp and played a strange, unsettled music that hovered between two modes. Then he began:

After the Cattle Raid of Cooley, Cuchulainn rested from his triumph. But Queen Medbh brooded on her defeat and plotted revenge on him. She summoned to her court druids from Alba, and wizards and sorcerers from eastern lands. Then she found three misshapen sisters, daughters of Calatin, the druid, whose sons had been killed by Cuchulainn. She took the sisters and had them trained in the black arts. At the same time she incited her two great warriors Lughaid and Erc, whose fathers had been killed by Cuchulainn, to raise an army against the Ulster hero.

When news of Medbh's plans reached Conchobar, he sent in haste to Cuchulainn, ordering him to come to the palace. When the king's messenger arrived, Cuchulainn was standing on the green before his house, shooting at birds with slingshots and missing his aim. He listened to the orders of the king with a heavy heart, for already he felt his powers beginning to desert him. Nevertheless he went with the messenger to Emain Macha.

As soon as Cuchulainn reached the palace, Medbh let loose the three black-hearted sisters. Raven-formed, they flew to the court and fluttered down on the great plain. Then they conjured a phantom army out of leaves and grasses, filling the air outside the palace with the noise of battle – loud trumpet-blasts, the clashing of weapons, shrieking of women, the crackling of fires and the cries of warriors.

Beguiled by this magic, Cuchulainn leaped up and reached for his sword. But Cathbad the druid called out sharply, forbidding him to go. 'The sound of warfare is an illusion sent to trick you,' he said. 'Wait safely in the castle, for such an illusion can only hold for three days. After that it will fade.'

But Cuchulainn looked out and his mind was gripped by the swirl of the phantom battle. He heard the frail melody of harpstrings floating among the shrieks and clashes, moans and hubbub of the fighting. Such hypnotic music, swelling through the sounds of the commotion, maddened him. He thought it was the son of Mangur playing his chieftain's harp to lay a magic on the army. He knew that to hear such magic was forbidden him. He recognized the breaking of this *geis* as a second sign of weakness.

Seeing he was maddened by the sounds, the wise men of the court ordered that he be taken secretly by night to the Valley of the Deaf, where he would be unable to hear the battle. A company from the household went with him, including minstrels and poets whose task was to distract him. There, in the castle, he rested safely for a day. But on the second day the hag-like sisters found him and, as the third day dawned, once again raised their battle enchantment around the fortress walls.

Then one of them took on the likeness of the maiden, Niamh, and entering the stronghold, came to Cuchulainn and berated him for not defending the province. Cuchulainn was taken aback, for Niamh was one of the women who had made him swear to remain inside. Madness came on him, and crying out that he would never again trust a woman, he seized his weapons and followed the wraith-like figure of Niamh out of the fort.

At once he found himself in a swirling fog in which images of comrades real or imagined came towards him or were snatched away. When Niamh herself ran to him in the fog and begged him to hold back and resist the delusions, Cuchulainn thrust her aside, vowing he would go out and defend Ulster whatever the cost.

He called for Laeg, his charioteer, to fetch his horses, the Black of Saingliu and the Grey of Macha. But when he tried to yoke the Grey to the chariot, the horse reared up, rolled his eyes, and ran off. Laeg chased after him and brought him back, but when Cuchulainn put his hand on the horse, tears of blood ran from its eyes. Nevertheless Cuchulainn yoked him to the chariot and climbed in.

As the great hero turned his chariot, fifty queens who had come from Emain Macha to be with him let out a great cry, for they knew they would never see him again. Their wailing pierced through the fog and mingled with the strange shapes and apparitions, muffled sounds and visions that began to come to him from every side. As he drove away, he looked back at the castle and thought he saw black smoke and flame streaming from is ramparts. Then he thought he saw the headless body of his wife Emer fall burning from the castle wall. He looked again, and saw the castle standing unharmed as before.

Turning his back on Emain, Cuchulainn rode with Laeg over tree-fringed hills and plains heavy with lowering skies, past fist-headed trees that came at them through skirls of fog, until they reached a dark-grassed meadow. There they saw a ford and a woman kneeling by it, washing the clothes and arms of a warrior. The water dripping from the clothes was red with blood and Cuchulainn saw that they were his own clothes that she was washing.

'Who is that woman?' he asked Laeg.

Laeg answered: 'She is the Washer of the Ford. She washes the clothes and arms of those who are about to die.' He broke off, his voice choking. Then he said: 'O Cuchulainn, let us turn back while there is still time!'

But Cuchulainn refused and made Laeg drive on, and as they came up to the ford the woman vanished.

They crossed the ford and took a narrow stony track between two fields. There they came upon three old crones, each blind in the left eye, sitting round a fire. They were cooking dog meat on spits of rowan wood. Cuchulainn went to pass by them, for it was taboo to him to eat the flesh of his own namesake. But the crones called out to him:

'Come and eat with us, Cuchulainn.'

'I will not,' he replied.

Nevertheless the women compelled him to go to them, reminding him that he was also under *geis* to accept food offered to him at the roadside.

Then one of the women held out a joint of the roast and gave it to him. Cuchulainn took it in his left hand and ate some of it. But as he climbed back into the chariot he felt the left side of his body suddenly become weak.

They drove on and came at last to Slieve Fuad where Medbh's army was encamped. Erc looked up and saw the hero hurtling towards them, standing upright in his chariot, his hair streaming out like rays from his head.

'Prepare yourselves,' he shouted, 'Cuchulainn is coming.'

At his shout, the phalanx raised a wall of linked shields as stout as a castle's ramparts, but Cuchulainn charged at them and performed his three great thunder-feats, slashing through their bodies with sword and spear until the ground was strewn with their scattered limbs.

He was shouting to Lugh to drive on, when a white-robed druid ran up and demanded his spear.

'You have less need of it than I,' replied Cuchulainn, 'for the armies of Medbh are hard upon me.'

'If you refuse to give it to me, I will put the power of satire on you,' cried the druid in a loud voice. In answer Cuchulainn threw it end-first at the man's head. He threw it with such force that it went right through the man's skull and sliced through the skulls of nine Connacht warriors, before landing quivering in the blood-stained grass. Immediately Lugaid, the army captain, ran and picked it up. Then he hurled it back at Cuchulainn with all his might. The spear hurtled towards the chariot, missed Cuchulainn and instead struck Laeg. The charioteer fell backwards, his entrails spilling from his body, and died in agony in

Cuchulainn's arms.

In a frenzy of rage and anguish, Cuchulainn took the reins himself and made to drive off again, but as he turned the chariot a second druid came running up, demanding another spear.

'If you refuse to give it to me I will curse Ulster with a satire,' he cried defiantly.

In answer, Cuchulainn hurled his second spear through the druid's head, and again it shot through the druid's skull and went on to kill nine of the enemy behind him.

As it lay quivering in the blooded grass, the chieftain Erc ran and picked it up and flung it back at Cuchulainn. The spear missed Cuchulainn but, instead, pierced his horse, the Grey of Macha. Cuchulainn snatched the spear out of the horse and tried to staunch the flow of blood, but the anguished creature broke violently away and galloped into the battlefield, dragging half the yoke behind him.

Then Cuchulainn drove his chariot in a fury through the host, drawn by the Black of Saingliu and dealing slaughter as he went. But when his chariot wheels stalled on a heap of corpses, a third druid ran up, demanding that he hand over his last spear. A third time Cuchulainn refused.

'Then I will curse Ulster!' cried the druid.

'I have already paid for the honour of Ulster!'

'Then I will curse your people!' said the druid.

In answer Cuchulainn flung his last spear handle-first through the druid's head and this time the spear sliced through three lots of nine men.

But Lugaid was waiting. He ran and picked up the spear and sent it speeding back at Cuchulainn with unerring aim. This time it met its mark. It ripped open Cuchulainn's belly so that he fell forward in the chariot.

For a while the hero lay there unmoving. Then, with blood pouring from his wounds, he slowly raised himself up and, holding his flesh and guts together, pitched himself out of the chariot and onto the ground. Watched by the warriors, he staggered to a nearby lake. After he had drunk from the lake, he began dragging himself towards an ancient pillar stone. When he reached it he pulled himself up and lashed his belt tightly around his gaping body and the stone. Then he raised his head and faced the enemy.

By now, a host of Connacht warriors had gathered round him. A long time they stood, watching as the hero's face slowly paled in the waning light of day. When at last he dropped his head and became motionless, a loud shriek split the silence and a jagged black raven flew down and alighted on his shoulder.

Bruach's voice broke. He bowed his head for a long time while we waited in silence. When at last he looked up, he said quietly:

'And so the Morrigan came to claim him at the end, for no one, not even a hero, can escape the fated moment of his death.' He paused.

'And if you understand that to leave this life is but to pass into another, you may stride towards your fate with equal fortitude.'

Then, lifting his harp onto his shoulders, he walked past the fire and into the night.

13
Níall and the Goddess of Sovereignty

'It is late,' said Bruach, 'and the shadows wait. In them you can fancy hideous beings lurk, seeking to fright or challenge us. Beings such as the *Cailleach*.'

He looked round at us, a red light in his eyes.

'Yes,' he said, 'the most fearful hag you could ever imagine! And you are right to fear her, for her powers are very great, greater than perhaps you know.'

He stood up and the red firelight ran down his staff.

'You have already met her, if you remember, for she is an aspect of the Dark Goddess. In the story of Cuchulainn, the Morrigan herself, terrible and beautiful as she is, appeared in Cailleach guise when she fooled the hero into healing her wounds.'

'She is the ancient one, the Challenger, the wise old crone. Like harsh winter in the eternal round of the seasons, she destroys and cleanses in order to prepare for rebirth and renewal. Some call her the Veiled One for, though she is hideous, her ugliness is a veil that covers her true face. We hate and fear her, but we need her. And so we must honour her. We must love her as the land itself, for she *is* the land. Our kings especially must love her, for in her hand she holds the gift of Sovereignty.'

'My story tonight concerns King Niall. Niall was great, as great as Cormac, and ruled from Tara. But first he suffered the fate of the king-child. As soon as was born he was put away, for his life was in danger. He was raised in safety by a poet-seer who taught him the hidden knowledge. And when he came of age, he returned to his father's palace to claim his rights. But such a story is timeless. It is the story of all kings and heroes. It is the story of those who must seek their destinies and, in seeking, face their challenges and win their rights.'

Then Bruach played a bold and melancholy air on his harp, an air of our land that brought strong tears to our eyes. It spoke of the rolling hills, the tilled fields, the mountains and the lakes. It spoke of the secret places beneath the hedgerows, and of the waste places – the chasms, the rocks and the marshland. As soon as he had made our hearts wide open to our beloved country, he put his harp aside.

'My tale begins after Niall had returned to the palace and claimed his place alongside his brothers,' he said.

Then he fixed us with eyes that glittered in the firelight.

One day the brothers all went out hunting together. They were hoping to bring down a deer, but when evening came they had only caught small game. Disappointed, they were just about to turn for home when they spotted a young fawn. Immediately they called up their hounds and chased after it. They were still pursuing it when darkness fell and they found themselves deep in the forest. Undaunted, they prepared to spend the night under the trees. They built a fire and roasted some of the game they had caught. Then they toasted each other with ale. When the ale ran out, they were still thirsty so one of the brothers, Fergus, offered to go and look for water.

He set off between the low-branched trees, stumbling over twigs and tree-roots as he went. The noises of the forest cracked around him – the scratching of small animals, the smack of falling branches, the creaking of trees, but no sound of water could he hear. He was beginning to despair when he saw a patch of silver ahead. He ran towards the light and found it was a moon-filled glade lying open to the sky. In the middle of it he could see the outline of a stone well. He started towards it, but as he did so a hunched figure limped towards him out of the shadows. He drew back in fright, for he saw it was a hideous old woman. A shaft of moonlight fell across her face, and Fergus froze. For her eyes stared horribly, each black pupil reflecting the cold disc of the moon, her skin was gnarled and covered with warts, bristles sprouted from her chin, and strands of black hair hung from her scalp like a horse's tail. She leered at him and in the split of her mouth were yellow teeth, savage and pointed. As soon as he had recovered from the fright, Fergus calmed himself and tried again to approach the well. But the hag let out a scream, harsh and grating as a crow's cry, and her eyes flamed. Fergus backed away.

'Why, woman, you are foul!' he said, his body shaking with fear.

She gave no answer.

'Do you guard the well?'

She nodded.

'May I have some water?'

In answer the woman came towards him and croaked: 'Only if you take me in your arms and kiss me.'

Fergus drew away in horror.

'Never!' he said.

'Then you shall go thirsty!'

'I would sooner die of thirst than think of kissing you!' he said.

At that she let out a deep-throated cackle and the prince began to run. He could hear her wheezy laughter following him as he fled back to the fire where his brothers waited.

Seeing his fear and panic, they asked what wild animal had chased him. When he told them what had happened they laughed scornfully and jeered at him for letting an old hag prevent him from going to the well.

When they had laughed their fill, one of the other brothers offered to go. He set off boldly with his head high while the others waited expectantly. But before many minutes had passed, he, too, came running back looking as if the hounds of hell were after him. And so it was with all the brothers. Each was greeted by the hag and chose to flee rather than kiss her until, finally, it was Niall's turn.

Taking his courage in his hands, Niall set out in the faint moonlight and strode towards the clearing. As before, the old woman loomed out of the blackness and hissed. She came so near that he could smell her foul breath. He saw the wisps of hair hanging from her chin, the warty skin wobbling on her cheeks and the liquid oozing from her nose and eyes.

'It is the same for you as for the others,' she said, 'the price of water is a kiss!' Then she gave a great squawk of laughter.

Niall forced himself to go towards her. He closed his eyes and held out his arms. As he felt her near, he put his arms around her. When he met her lips, instead of being dry and cracked as he expected, he found they were full and smooth. At the same time, instead of the stench he had steeled himself to endure, a sweet perfume rose in his nostrils. Astonished, he opened his eyes and found that the hag he thought he held had become the most beautiful and beguiling maiden he had ever seen. Her skin was smooth and white as winter snow, her arms were shapely and strong, her hands were delicate, her fingers slender, her legs perfectly formed. She had gold shoes on her feet and a purple cloak round her shoulders clasped with a silver brooch. She looked at him with large and sorrowing eyes.

'Indeed you are a fair woman!' said Niall in wonder, as he gazed on her.

She smiled.

'Who are you?' he asked.

In answer, she drew away from him, and light streamed out from her so that he feared to touch her. In a voice like the sound of flowing water, she said: 'My name is Sovereignty. I rule the land. Its wind is my breath, its rivers are my tears, its earth is my body and its caves are my womb.'

She came towards Niall and her beautiful eyes searched his.

'In my hand also is its kingship. And you are the one of my choosing,' she said.

Then she led him to the well and filled his pitcher with water.

'This is for you, Niall,' she said. 'And, because you did not shrink from embracing me in my ugliness, because you were bold enough to obey me, and because you had the strength to withstand my test, you are worthy of the kingship of this land.'

She handed him the pitcher.

'And now I make this pledge that you and your sons will rule over Erin forever.'

Then she told him to return to his brothers but not to give them any water until they had sworn him their allegiance. And in token of such an oath, she said, he might raise his weapon a hand's span above theirs when they reached home.

When Niall returned to his brothers, his face was shining. He told them his story and asked them to give him their allegiance as Sovereignty had instructed him. After they had sworn their oaths, he gave them the water from the pitcher, and in their mouths it tasted sweet as rose petals.

Next morning the five sons returned home to their father. As they approached the court they lifted their weapons in salute, but Niall lifted his a hand's span higher. The queen asked why Brian, the eldest, had not held his highest. Her sons told her that they had yielded the sovereignty to Niall and had pledged themselves to him with oaths. All the court fell silent at their words. But after they had heard the story, Sithchenn the seer came forward and declared that the brothers had wisely forfeited their rights to the throne and that Niall was now the true and acknowledged king.

Bruach gave a regal flourish on his harp. Then he glanced up quickly, catching the look of the men among us.

'How many of you,' he asked, 'would have taken such a hag into your arms?'

In answer the men began muttering among themselves. The fili's voice cut through their boasting.

'Ah, some of you think you would be man enough, do you?'

He paused, sweeping his pale blue eyes slowly round the gathering.

'Then consider this. How many of you have enough love for

the land, its warts and wrinkles, its waste places, its pits and caves? And how many of you care for the struggles of its people?'

He paused again. When no one answered he said in a voice so soft it seemed to whisper to our very souls: 'For that is the price of kingship.'

14
Finn and the Salmon of Wisdom

'Fish are the treasures of the waters,' said Bruach.

We were sitting together, looking into a deep pool.

'But none are as precious as the salmon, because of its remarkable endurance. For it swims for miles upstream to find its spawning ground. Which is why it has been chosen by the gods to carry the deepest wisdom.'

He smiled.

'But what the salmon offers is not of this world, it is the power of inner vision which comes from the Otherworld, the world of spirit.'

A fish flicked towards the surface of the water and disappeared again.

'What is that power?' I asked.

'It is the power of *imbas*,' replied the fili, 'the inspiration which comes from poetry. Like the salmon itself, it lurks in the well-springs of the soul – and is very hard to catch.'

He looked again at the water.

'But catch it you must,' he said, turning towards me, 'if you are to become a seer!'

As he said these words, a thrill ran through my heart. A vision sprang up in my mind. I saw myself dressed in flowing robes, a beard covering my chin and a hazel staff in my hand.

'Will I really be a seer?' I asked.

'You have some of the Knowing already,' he answered, 'and there is much that you will learn in your training.'

He looked at me, his pale eyes intense.

'But there are some things that cannot be learned with the mind,' he said.

I let my eyes rest on the water.

'There are three ways of summoning *imbas* that the seer must know,' he said. 'Although you have not yet undergone your bardic training, these powers may already be yours.'

He looked up at the branches overhead and froze suddenly, listening intently. All I could hear was a blackbird fluting and fluttering his wings. We were both silent for a while. Then he continued: 'The first is the power of prophetic dream. The second is the power of knowledge by touch.'

Bruach paused. 'And the third is the power of knowledge through inspiration.' He looked at me intently.

'And that is the power I think you have already,' he said, 'for it comes from composing poetry.'

'What makes you think I have this power?' I asked.

'Because, soon after I came to this village, I heard you speak an invocation to the Well of Wisdom.'

He stroked his staff.

'In your poem was more power and knowledge than I think you had before you wrote it,' he said.

I thought of the poem. I remembered speaking it to my little harp and shivering when I spoke the words of power. I remembered fearing that I had called up forces beyond my understanding.

'That power,' said the fili, 'is the power of *imbas*, of which I have already spoken, and it comes from the Salmon of Knowledge. But the Salmon gives itself where it will and to whom it pleases, and the patience of a lifetime cannot earn a man such knowledge.'

He smiled at me again.

'But once,' he said, 'there was a seer who devoted years of his life to catching it. You may have heard of him. His name was Finnegas and a young boy called Demna was sent to him for teaching and instruction.'

He began uncovering the harp.

'If this story is new to you,' he said, 'then you must hear it. But even if you know it well, listen again, for there is always new wisdom to be found within it.'

As he spoke he began to play a melody that I thought suited the harp best – a rippling watery music. After playing for a while, he began to speak in a far-away voice.

An old druid known as Finnegas or Finn the Seer, was sitting beside a deep pool on the banks of the Boyne. He had waited there for many years, while the river Boyne swirled past him, puckering with endless spirallings and patterns. But Finn ignored the river. Instead he spent his time gazing into the black bowl of the pool, seeking to penetrate its darkness. Sometimes he would glimpse a streak of silver mottled with spots of pink dart near the surface for a fleeting moment. Then he would sigh and think of the five sleek salmon lurking in its depths filled with the secret knowledge, feeding on the nuts of inspiration dropped by the nine great hazel trees that overhung the pool. He would think of the salmon eating the red-pink nuts and releasing their husks to float away on the five streams that ran out from the well.

The old man waited with the patience of age, for he had been given a prophecy that one called Finn was destined to taste the sacred salmon and become imbued with its wisdom and inspiration. This was the wisdom of illumination, a gift of the gods. And so the old man waited with trembling awe for this gift to become his own.

While he waited, the boy Demna was sent to him for instruction. The boy was sturdy, with a keen eye and unruly yellow locks. He told the seer that he knew the ways of the wood by heart, he had learned the tracks of animals, the songs of the birds and the properties of the trees.

The seer instructed him in the mystical knowledge. First he taught him the symbols of the ogham, grooving their shapes onto yew and hazel sticks. Then he made him learn the ancient stories, working them into verse and seeking poetic inspiration from them. He taught him the laws of the holy man, the shape changer, and how to take on the spirits of birds and fish and animals, to fight with the cunning of wolf nature and to struggle against hardship like the ancient salmon itself. He taught him how to read the flights of birds, how to raise mists over the army of an enemy and how to blemish a king's face by the power of satire.

Demna was an apt pupil and learned quickly. When the teaching was over for the day the young boy and the old man would sit and gaze into the pool together, watching for a streak of pink-flecked silver, and sometimes a salmon would leap into the air and hang in front of them, but would plunge back again before they had time to grasp it.

Then one morning the boy ran to the pool early and found

the old man just waking. He shouted out to him, for he saw that the thing had happened at last. A great sleek salmon had leaped from the pool and was lying on the banks of the river flapping its tail with the last of its strength. The seer could hardly contain his joy. He lifted the heavy fish into the boy's arms and told him to take it away and cook it, but he made him promise not to eat any of the fish until he had brought it back.

Soon the boy returned carrying the cooked fish. But there was something in the way he walked, something in the tilt of his head, that told the seer the boy had changed.

'Demna,' he said, 'did you eat any of the salmon while you were cooking it?'

'No,' replied the boy.

Then he began to test the boy with riddles.

'Tell me,' he said, 'what is brighter than the sun?'

'Wisdom from the hand of a god,' replied the boy.

'And what is faster than lightning?'

'Inspiration from the hand of a god,' said the boy.

Then Finnegas said again: 'Demna, have you eaten any of the salmon?'

'No,' said the boy, 'except that a blister rose on the skin and I pressed it down with my thumb, and then I put my thumb in my mouth because it was burning.'

'Is Demna your only name?' asked Finnegas.

'Yes,' said the boy, 'except that sometimes people call me Finn, because of my yellow hair.'

At this the old man sighed and tears came in his eyes.

'So,' he said softly, 'the gift was for you. The power of the gods has lighted on your shoulders, use it well,' and he touched the boy's head in blessing. Then Demna spoke this incantation.

Bruach paused and looked at me. Then he struck up a melody in the *geantrai*, the glad-strain, and I began to sing:

May-time, season of perfection.
The song of the blackbird overflows
in the last beam of the day.

The cuckoo cries its note,
heralding the summer.
Bitter weather is no more.

Summer is the summoner
of the winding stream. Lowing cows
seek out its waters, while the heather
spreads its tresses on the fields.

The harp of the wood sounds its music,
bringing perfect peace, while colours
shed their veils on every hill, a full mist
covering the lake ... ⑪

After I finished singing, Bruach took up the tale again.

And as the boy sang the old seer felt the stirring of joy in his heart. He felt the power of the god, which, though it had passed him by, had yet come close to him.

The fili put his harp aside.

'And after that time, whenever the boy put his thumb in his mouth and touched his tooth of wisdom, he was able to see visions. Whenever he chewed on it, he was able to summon the power of truth.

Bruach turned towards me.

'You will have heard of the boy,' he said, 'for he grew up to become Finn mac Cumhail, the great captain of the Fianna, the famous warrior band of Erin.'

Bruach leaned forward and cupped some water in his hands.

'Once,' he said, 'you asked me where the Well of Wisdom could be found.'

He drank the water.

'Now I am asking *you* the same question. Where can such a well can be found?'

He looked at me expectantly.

I wanted to please him with a clever answer. But my mind suddenly became as blank and dark as the surface of the pool itself.

We sat in silence while he waited for my answer and I waited for the pool to clear.

At last, because I could think of nothing better, I said: 'I think the pool that is in front of us is the well.'

To my surprise he nodded encouragingly. Emboldened, I went on: 'And your staff is the hazel of inspiration.'

He nodded again. 'And what about the Salmon itself?' he asked.

I looked around me. I could see nothing that seemed a symbol for the salmon. I closed my eyes and stopped thinking of the salmon and thought of its knowledge and wisdom instead.

Suddenly I looked at Bruach.

'Your teaching and the inner knowing it awakes in me,' I said. 'That is the Salmon.'

15
Oisin goes to the Land of Youth

Druach stood before us, fierce in the firelight.

'As this is my last story before I leave you,' he said, 'I have chosen to take you to another land.'

He gripped his staff.

'Indeed, it could be argued that every story takes you there. But tonight I will speak of it plainly.'

He bent over his harp and played a sweet, silvery tune upon it, like the music of the *sidhe.*

'There is a land that calls to us,' he said. 'It is *Tir na n'Og*, the Land of Youth. Sometimes it is found far across the sea, and at other times on islands deep beneath the waters. It is a mystical realm, a land of enchantment that offers us the riches of the soul – some would say our very soul itself. Brave men and heroes have set out to find it, seeking to carry back its treasures. Seers have journeyed there to find its power and its wisdom. But for the ordinary mortal there is danger, for the call of the land is strong and the faerie women who inhabit it are beautiful and alluring. Sometimes they come here and offer to take us to their paradise – and it is tempting to go with them. But what do we know about it? Are there riches to be found there, or are its pleasures only an illusion?'

Plucking a few more silvery notes from his harp, he began to tell the story:

It was early one summer morning, when the great chieftain Finn mac Cumhail with his brave war band, the Fianna, were out hunting in the mountains of Kerry. The air was sharp and the hounds had yet to pick up a scent. Wisps and wraiths of mist floated before them like a silvery landscape and the air was so fragile they should have known that the Otherworld was hovering near. As they approached Lough Lein they reined in their horses and gazed across its surface. It lay spread out before them shimmering and wrinkling like the filmy cloak of the sea-god himself. Then suddenly, a flash of pale sun broke through the mist and they saw a bright figure far out across the water.

As the figure came nearer they saw what it was – a slip of a young woman riding a white horse across the very tips of the waves. The sun coming up for the morning haloed her hair in a shining ball, and her tresses went streaming from her head like golden tendrils. The men of the Fianna drew in their breath and watched in wonder as she came towards them.

A gold band sat upon her head like a crown, while a silk cloak sprinkled with red gold stars flew like a cloud from her shoulders. Her eyes were blue as the mountain flower and her cheeks soft and pink like the petals of the wild rose. Her horse was saddled and bridled in pure gold – even its hooves were shod with gold and, as she rode, they struck bright sparks from the tumbling waves. When the woman drew near, a perfume wafted before her. It was as if she brought with her all the spices of the south.

The woman halted in front of Finn but kept astride her horse.

'Oh, King of the Fianna,' she said, 'I have travelled far for the sake of love.'

'Who are you?' asked Finn 'and from what land do you come?'

'My name has been spoken by the lips of bards, my songs have been sung to the sound of harps. My name is Niamh, the Golden-haired, and my father is King of *Tír na n'Og*, the Land of Youth.'

The men, who were already lost in wonder, marvelled even more when they heard her words, for this was a land they had heard of and, indeed, all longed for, but few had ever been there or knew whether it existed.

But Finn, the wily, faced her boldly, being neither in love with the woman, nor yet in awe of her.

'What errand makes you travel so far?' he asked her, his voice barbed like a ready spear, 'has a husband betrayed you perhaps or brought you grief?'

'I have no husband,' replied the woman, 'I have refused all suitors, for my heart is set on your son.'

'Lady, which of my brave sons has provoked such love?' asked Finn.

Niamh looked at the young warrior waiting on his horse beside Finn. She looked at his broad-shoulders, his hair like the waterfall and his trim beard, and she saw the gleam of his bronze arms showing beneath his crimson cloak.

'It is your son Oisin, the brave warrior and gentle bard of the land,' she said. 'It is he who has stolen my heart and brought me this far across the seas.'

A blade of fear touched the great captain and his heart began to beat with dread. 'Tell me,' he said, 'why of all the noble warriors of this land, it is my son Oisin that you have set your heart on?'

The woman looked the brave knight up and down who still sat unmoving upon his horse.

'It is because of the report of his great boldness, his deeds and his valour. His fame has reached like the bellow of a boar's horn across the sea, and has come to the ears of the immortal ones who dwell in *Tir na n'Og*,' she said. 'And though the finest and noblest princes of the land have laid their wealth before me and begged for my hand, I refused them all because of the longing that I have for your son.'

As she spoke, her words danced in the young man's heart; the deep wells of her eyes, the golden web of her hair, and the perfume that breathed about her, all these things held him as if by a spell. Before he could stop himself, he had climbed from his horse and gone towards her.

'Lady,' he said, 'I swear to you, of all the women in the world, you are the darling of my heart. You are my own soul come to me, and my only wife on this earth!'

The woman smiled and threw back her head. From her white throat came a soft humming that filled the air. The warriors looked at her in wonder. For such singing had never been heard before in all the land of Erin. It was like the music of the birds of Cliodna in full-throat, like the pale-robed goddess singing creation into being.

> There is a land incomparable in beauty,
> where the sea lifts silver waves against the sand,
> where white-maned horses of Manannan rear and glisten,
> fields of emerald stretch out on either hand.
>
> A sacred land where soft streams soothe the spirit,
> death is banished, grief and sickness have no hold.
> A wondrous land that thrills with song and sings forever,

skies are azure and the meadows yellow-robed.

A golden land of summer everlasting,
where heroes feast and daring tales are told,
a land where trees hold in their branches healing apples,
where all are beautiful and youthful, none grows old.

O come with me, Oisin, my mortal darling,
claim the lordship of that rich enchanted land,
for I, the gentle faerie Niamh – its golden princess,
ever young and lovely, offer you my hand ... ⑫

The power of the faerie maiden, her fragrance, and her song, filled his head like a long wild call, the call of the land itself. The words bursting from his mouth, Oisin cried out:

'Lady, I will come with you!'

He ran and kissed his father and hugged each of his comrades in turn. Then he sprang up on the beautiful white horse and sat behind Niamh with his arms around her waist. She touched its flank with her jewelled spur and the horse gave three great neighing cries, shook its mane and shot across the water like a streak of flame.

But Finn uttered a great shout of grief, a long wail that reached across the lake and followed after Oisin: 'My son so fair and brave, will I never see you again! It breaks my heart to lose so dear a son!'

Then he wept long and bitterly for Oisin, and cursed the day the faerie woman thought to come from the land of *Tir na n'Og* to claim him.

But Oisin was already far out at sea, holding tight to Niamh.

They were travelling towards the islands of the west with the speed of Manannan's ship itself. As they journeyed, many wondrous sights passed by them faster than a flash of foam – white-walled cities, snow-touched mountains gilded by the sun, castles perched like crows on rocky hillsides, and palaces with bronze cupolas like burning helmets. They also saw strange animals; a deer yellow as the sun at noon, bounding across a green field, and a white hound, red-eared, chasing after it. They passed strange people; a maiden with a golden apple in her hand riding across the waves on a brown horse, and a young warrior flying after her, crimson robes stretched out like wings behind him and a sword blade glittering in his hand.

'Who are the pair of riders?' asked Oisin.

'Ask no questions until we reach the Land of Youth,' replied Niamh, 'for nothing you see comes near the glories of that land.'

So Oisin kept his tongue to himself while they rode on. Day and night they travelled, neither stopping nor speaking, until all at once the huddling waves reared up in front of them and the sky fell into blackness. Red shafts of lightning stabbed through the clouds and rain fell on them like fine sharp arrows. Oisin and Niamh cowered into the damp mane of the horse while the storm god raged. Then all at once the rain stopped and a clear bright jewel of a sun struck through the clouds. It lit up a wondrous island that was spread out before them with green plains running away on either side and, in the middle of it, a shining castle.

'What is this land?' asked Oisin.

'The Land of Youth,' Niamh replied.

With that she brought the horse to a halt upon the green. Even before they could dismount, a host of warriors in burnished armour and a party of maidens dressed in silk garments came rushing out to welcome them. The king himself in great magnificence rode to meet them with the queen beside him, young and fair as a summer rose.

The king came up to Oisin: 'A hundred thousand welcomes!' he said, 'and long may you live among us. May this kingdom give you every pleasure you desire, for this is the land of which the bards tell, the land they celebrate in poetry and song.'

Oisin thanked the king for his welcome. Then he and Niamh were taken into the palace along with the king and all his people, where they found a great feast had been laid out for them. But this was only the beginning. For the feasting and dancing and celebrating carried on for ten days and nights, and great joy and gladness was had in honour of the couple's wedding.

In that land, just as Niamh promised, Oisin had everything he could desire – the finest horses and chariots, the rarest food, the choicest wines, the richest garments, the pleasures of the hunt and, besides all this, the love of the beautiful Niamh herself. But, happy though he was most of the time, there was one thing that gave him sadness – the thought of Finn and the Fianna and the longing to see them again. At last the longing became so strong that he went to Niamh and told her that he must return to his old land. Niamh's beautiful face turned pale when she heard his words. But he said he would only be gone a short time and straight afterwards would return.

'I cannot hold you back if your heart is set on it,' she said through her tears, 'But the journey is dangerous and the thought of it fills me with great fear.'

Oisin comforted her and said he would ride the very same

horse that carried them both so bravely, and would come swiftly home as soon as he had seen his comrades.

'You must promise me one thing,' said Niamh through her tears. 'In all the time you are in Erin, you must not once climb down from your horse or let any part of you touch the ground, for otherwise you will never be able to return.'

Oisin promised to do as she said and made ready for his journey. Then he took Niamh in his arms and kissed her, mounted his horse and set off across the white-waved sea.

The journey seemed long without Niamh, and the wonders that he passed less marvellous to him than before. But at last, after several days' travel, his heart leaped high within him as he saw, far off, the dim green coast of Erin. The horse slackened pace when they reached the shore and trotted up the beach while Oisin stayed in the saddle, searching anxiously for signs of his old comrades.

He had not long arrived before a cavalcade of men and women came into view. They marched up to the unknown rider and greeted him, marvelling at his great size and strength. Oisin, for his part, was astonished at their tiny stature and the strange clothes they were wearing. He began to ask about Finn and the Fianna. The people looked puzzled at his questions. Some said they had heard of such a man, but that he lived a long time ago, while others thought he was a character in story.

With fear growing in his heart, Oisin turned his horse and set out towards Leinster. He galloped all the way without stopping until he came to Finn's rath in Dun Aileann. There he found the hall decayed, its walls clothed in briars and wild grasses. Oisin gave a great and terrible cry, calling for Finn and the Fianna, but his voice echoed among the stones and fell away down the hillside.

He cried again but no answering call came from the deserted rath. Then, throwing up his arms, he called out wildly all the names of the Fianna one by one. He even called the names of Finn's hounds, Bran and Skolawn, but there was still no answer.

Then a horror came on him and he rode wildly out of the dun as if fleeing an enchantment. He galloped eastwards until he came to the Thrushes' Glen. There he slowed, for he saw a group of men heaving at a huge boulder. It seemed to him child's play to move such a stone. He went over to them meaning to enquire again about the Fianna. Seeing they were intent on their work, he leaned down from his horse and heaved at the stone, hurling it far across the field. But he leaned down so far, the girth of his saddle broke and pitched him to the earth.

As soon as Oisin's body touched the ground, a terrible transformation came over him. His skin began to shrivel like paper in a fire, his golden hair turned silver and his eyes shrank into his head. Three hundred years had come upon him in an instant making him feeble and powerless. He groaned and struggled to get up, but it was too late. The terrified men stood rooted, appalled by the change that had come upon him, while the horse reared up in panic and galloped back, riderless, across the sea.

Bruach gave a strange half smile. He began running his nails up and down the strings of his harp, making a whistling sound. Then he softened the sound, thinning it until it blew away like the wind. At last, flinging out a handful of notes like a scatter of dry leaves, he packed up his harp and left us to our Otherworldly dreams.

16
The Coming of Adzed Head

The next day I was up early and waiting for Bruach in the wood.

It was our last morning together. He came and sat beside me.

'There was more to tell about Oisin last night,' he said, 'But it has not yet come to pass for he is still in the Land of Youth.'

I started with surprise at his words and he put his hand on my shoulder.

'Time is not what it seems,' he said, 'And to a seer, the order of events is less important than the events themselves. Every event, every happening is harnessed to the wheel of Fate, and because the wheel is always turning each has its time again.'

He drew an ogham sign in the bracken.

'When Oisin returns to Erin, three hundred years will indeed have passed, though in the Otherworld it appears to him like a few short years. And though his falling from the horse seems a cruel accident, nevertheless it is his fate.'

He looked at me intently and this time I found that I could hold his gaze.

'The small, weak men he found when he came back, are the race that will come after us,' he said.

A far-away look came into his eyes as if he was seeing visions.

'A black-winged people, like a flock of crows will come. They will seem at first like scavengers, come to strip us of our bounty. At their head is a strange man who carries a curve-headed staff of power that is unknown to us. He comes to do battle with our ancient knowing. Yet it is Oisin's destiny to meet him.'

He drew another ogham symbol in the bracken and again stared sightlessly at the thicket before him.

'They will call the man Adzed Head, because of the shaving of his hair. He will ask Oisin about the Fianna. And Oisin will live long enough to tell him the old tales.'

Bruach frowned.

'Then the man will worry that the old tales will overcome his power.'

He closed his eyes.

'But I see him again,' he said, 'kneeling down, consulting with his spirits.'

He sighed and tears gathered in his eyes.

'They are allowing our Knowing,' he said.

He was silent for a long time, writing further symbols in the soil beneath the bracken. When he looked up again I saw in his eyes what had made me fearful of him. It was his knowledge of the endlessness of time, of other forms and worlds, of the dark wellsprings of poetic truth. Now as I looked fearlessly into his eyes, his words rose in my mind. They came to me without his speaking.

'Remember, Magor, the Sacred Word waits, buried within the stories.'

His eyes darkened and I saw a flash of light deep within them.

'But with the turning of the wheel it will be released once more.'

As I heard these words, my own eyes blurred with tears. I thought of the Word that needed to be kept and held. I felt its burden and I felt its joy. I let my tears flow.

When I opened them again, I saw he was smiling down at me. I smiled back through my tears. Then he touched my head with his staff, turned and walked quickly away through the wood.

As soon as he was out of sight I heard a burst of music. I looked up and saw a gold-beaked blackbird sitting on the branch above me. It was pouring from its throat a rich and liquid melody. I sat and listened. And for the first time – or so it seemed to me, I began to understand.

ALBA

Alba is the Celtic name for Scotland. Although Scotland shares some of the Irish myths, particularly those of the Fenian cycle (known in Scotland as the Ossian cycle), many of their stories have come from the rich heritage of Scottish ballads handed down orally and collected by Professor Francis James Child in *The English and Scottish Popular Ballads*, 5 volumes, Boston 1882–98, Dover 1965. They are currently being reprinted in two volumes by Loomis House Press.

The story of Diarmaid and Grainne is claimed by both Ireland and Scotland. The version given here draws on some of the Scottish texts found in *Popular Tales of the West Highlands* by J. F. Campbell.

Prologue

17

Three Harpers on the Island of Rum

On Rum, an island of the Inner Hebrides
there is a cave round which the water sucks and leaps
and at the cave's mouth, washed by waves, a wrecked
fishing smack lies jewelled with limpet shells.
And from the cave's mouth on a clear day you can just descry
the outline of the Cuillin Hills upon the Isle of Skye.

Now it's a long time since this story came to pass
but once three galleys put out from three islands round
And moored together in a creek on Rum,
And three crews gathered in the cave's great mouth.

Now each crew had a harper and these bards
by fingering their harps within the cave
set off such magic echoes that the sound
shivered like a shaft of sunlight flashing round
– and each man listening wept as if his own lost self he'd found.

All night the powerful harping wove its magic
until at dawn the harps at last fell still
And with the spell still hanging in the air
the listeners asked the harpers what inspired their skill.

Said the First Harper:
Many moons ago
My mother gathered herbs upon the hills,
Enquired their properties and learned their arts
for healing battle wounds and the hearts hurts.
And I, her boy, received this Knowledge from her -

Said the Second Harper:
On a day,
herding a widow's cow in a deserted place
I saw an ancient solitary oak
sporting a bird's nest in its branches.
So I gathered worms and climbed the tree
eager to feed the waiting chicks.
The nest was empty. All at once I felt
a thought, a sadness, come into my heart.

Said the Third Harper:
Once there was a boat
Sailing towards our creek, a woman was on board
singing a strange song from another shore.
The song has called to me. My fingers ache
to play it and by playing it to reach the other shore.

'And these things make you into harpers,'
said the Listeners.
'They make us like little children,'
said the bard. ⑬ (Instrumental)

The whole cave was illumined with candles. Every niche and crevice held a flickering flame. Boughs of hawthorn and apple lay like offerings at the entrance. The three harpers who had announced themselves in poetry, sat together on three rush seats. They were waiting to tell their stories for, as was the yearly custom, this was a bardic competition. As they waited, each dreamed that the silver cup might become their own, and that they might 'ascend the bardic chair', and entertain the crowd with music and story throughout the night. Well might they desire this prize for with it came high honour and an invitation to every court throughout the land of Alba.

18
The Ballad of Tam Lín

The First Harper was dressed in a rich yellow cloak lined with soft kidskin. His hair was black and he had a short beard. He strode to the centre of the cave, carrying his stout harp, which he placed with care and elegance on the rough floor. A huge opal gleamed like an eye from the top of the thick, curved pillar. With a deft movement, the harper swept his cloak behind his shoulders, bent over his harp and drew a rippling flourish from it. He eyed the crowd and spoke in sonorous tones:

As all men here will know, there are two kinds of women, the wicked and the good. And a man's fate is determined by how far he is able to escape the one and discover the other. The story that I have for you tells of a man who falls prey to the one and is obliged to throw himself on the mercy of the other in order to escape the pangs of Hell. If this seems like riddling speech to you, the ballad will make all clear. But before I begin, I will tell you that the first kind of woman is an Otherworldly one and comes from the Land of Faerie, a land of rare promise that lures to its luminous shores the soul of many a worthy man. But it is a treacherous land, a land from where few return – for the returning is both painful and dangerous. So let this tale act as a warning to you all. But, before I begin, let me say that, familiar though the story may be, the rhyming of it is my own and the telling of it requires singing with musical accompaniment throughout. With that the First Harper began playing an air in the high modal style and after a few bars his rich voice rose above it:

Beware you maidens of Carterhaugh
of binding your golden hair,
of clothing yourself in long green skirts
and going to the pinewood there.

For the guardian of the pinewood
he is an elfin knave
and whether a maid will give or no
her golden ring he'll have.

But no brave maid of Carterhaugh
that enters the pinewood there
will travel back a maid again
or keep her honour dear.

Then Janet binds on her long green skirt
and twists it above her knee,
and boldly sets out for Carterhaugh
to see what she shall see.

Her hair is braided upon her head
and her steps are proud and high,
as she comes to the well at Carterhaugh
with a white rose tree hard by.

A white horse is waiting by the well
and no knave can she see,
But when she plucks a double rose
out of the earth comes he.

Oh why have you pulled my rose, Janet,
and why have you snapped my wand
and why have you come to Carterhaugh
when I never gave command?

Then Janet made answer to Tam Lin
as bold as brass was she
My father is lord of Carterhaugh
and has given the wood to me.

Though boldly, boldly has she come
and spoken aye so free
when fair young Janet reaches home
no longer a maid is she.

Four and twenty of her maids
are playing a game of chess
when Janet comes among them
her face is green as glass.

Alas, alas, sweet Janet fair
and who shall take the blame
what man has got you so soon with child
and who shall give him name.

A fairy lord has lain with me,
it is a fairy's child,
when that I plucked a double rose
that grew so sweet and wild.

My lord he rides a milk-white horse
swifter than the wind
its hooves are shod with silver
with heels of gold behind.

Janet puts on her long green skirt
and binds up her golden hair
and she has gone to Carterhaugh
to see if her knight is there.

She comes up to the fairy well
a double rose plucks she
and when Tam Lin comes close he says
I never summoned thee.

Oh why do you pull the rose, my love
Oh why do you make so free
And why do you seek to kill the child
That you have made with me?

For know you not I was a man
and hunted on the hill
the Queen of Faerie snatched me up
when from my horse I fell.

Though faerie land is fair and green
a pretty place to dwell,
yet at the end of seven years
we pay a tithe to hell.

Tonight is Halloween, my love
and I would wager thee
the father of your unborn child
the tithe to hell will be.

But you may save me if you will
and all will come aright
If you will birth and swaddle me
at the mid hour of night.

You must wait at the crossroads
and never so bold and brave
but you must hold me fast my love
if your bonnie bairn you'd have.

And when the Fairy troop are come
these tokens you will find,
let pass the black horse and the brown
the white horse will be mine.

My right hand will be gloved, my love
my left hand will be bare,
my bonnet will be lifted up
and down will flow my hair.

And if you snatch me from my horse
when faery bridles sound
and hold me fast through every change
your true love you will find.

I'll change into a hissing snake,
a bear, and next a lion,
then I'll become a red-hot rod
and after, a burning iron.

But you must dip me in some milk
and after in the well,
then take me out a naked knight
and wrap my body well.

So at the eerie dead of night
fair Janet went alone
and where two roads cross one on one
she waited in the gloom.

When at the stroke of midnight hour
the faery troop was come
she let the black horse gallop by
and after that the brown.

But when the milk-white steed came by
she seized its rider fair.
And while the fay troop surrounded her,
she clasped her lover near.

And he became a snake, a bear
and then a roaring lion
She held him as a red hot rod
and as a burning iron.

And then she dipped him in the milk
and after in the well
and when she covered up his flesh
she broke the faery spell.

Then forward came the Faery Queen
and angrily said she,
A curse on the maiden brave and bold
who set my Tam Lin free
for she has taken the fairest knight
in all my company.

If I had known, Tam Lin, she said
that you'd do this to me
I'd have plucked out your two grey eyes
and given you eyes of tree.

If I had known, Tam Lin, she said
that you'd leave me alone
I'd have plucked out your heart of flesh
and put in a heart of stone. ⑭

19
The Sea Maiden

The Second Harper stepped forward, carrying her little harp. She bowed low and her long hair swung in a twist of gold towards the cave floor. When she spoke, her voice was rich and silvery:

In the depths of the fish-bright sea around these blessed islands lie wondrous creatures, almost as ancient as the sea itself. Some can only be discovered in the depths of the ocean, but some have been seen on land for they are part human and can shape-change at will. Such creatures have haunted our shores, birthed mortal children and lent their magic to our race. The gift they bring is from the Mother, the all-embracing one, the wave-strewn sea itself, which formed and fosters us and carries in its depths our ancient half-forgotten memories.

Then she reached for her harp and spoke this invocation:

> Creature of wave and air,
> sleek-skinned Selchie. Woman-formed
> you walk with mortals; as a glittering silver seal
> you haunt the jewelled depths of ocean
> seeking within its halls the shining pearls
> of Knowledge and the Salmon Wisdom.
>
> Wrapped in the gleaming moon-pulled waters -

blue-dark mantle of the Mother,
fearless you tumble in her chambers
tasting her secrets and her mysteries;
or shimmer in the sun on wave-washed rocks
like mermaid's mirror in her flowing arms.

Older than time and tide the Mother's Knowing
Deeper than ocean bed the Wise One's Understanding. (15)

After speaking, she stood silent while we listened to the lilting rhythm of the waves licking at the rocky edges of the cave. Then, settling herself so that her long red dress fanned out like a mermaid's tale behind her, and her long fair hair fell to one side of her face, she took her harp on her knee, set her tiny fingers to the strings and started to play a dance-like melody. She tipped the harp as she played so that the jewels on its pillar and the gems on her fingers flashed in the reflected light. As the sounds dropped away into the depths of the cave, she began to speak:

On a warm fair night in Autumn with a harvest moon so low you could climb up with a ladder and pull it down, a fisherman was walking along the shore. He was looking out over the moon-flecked waters and crunching the shells beneath his toes. All at once he saw a haze of spray like the Milky Way itself, and it was made by a great splashing and commotion as had never been heard before in those parts. Coming closer he beheld a wonderful sight. A group of young women, naked as the day they were born, were sporting together in the brine. And the way they dived and twisted and plunged in the thrill of the water kept his two bright eyes wide-open in fascination.

But he was not long looking at them when they felt him there. And then wasn't there a panic and a rushing towards the rocks and a clambering and reaching for a pile of silver cloak skins as you never have seen the like. But in a flash the fisherman was there before them, snatching at the cloak skins with the best of them. And so it was that just before the last maid came to it, he had her cloak skin in his hand and would not give it back.

Bravely she stood in the water white and shivering, with her companions all gone from her, while her two breasts and all that was above and below them were a delight to him.

'Please,' she begged, reaching out her hand. 'Let me have my covering.'

'Not so!' said the man.

And what could she do but follow him back home, and all the while wailing and sighing after him. But in vain, for the fisherman, young and strong and supple as he was, and without a wife to comfort him, was heart-struck by his unexpected catch - this sleek-haired woman with the full, grey eyes. He set her in his house and locked the door. Then he climbed with the bundle up into the hay-house and, pulling out a brick, stuffed it behind. When that was done, the fisherman took it on himself to comfort the woman for her loss. Time passed and the maid became his wife and bore him two brave sons and a grey-eyed daughter.

It was on a day after this that the little one was sporting with her brothers and playing at Hide and Seek. When her turn came she climbed the hay-house high as she could go and what should she do but pull a brick out of place and there was a cloak of covering like the strands of the rainbow itself but tough and sinewy as well. The little one let it tumble out and went to fetch her mother.

'It feels rubbery like soft petals,' she said, 'and it wanted to stick on my hand.'

The mother held tight to the girl, and perhaps she slowed her steps a little, and perhaps there came a sudden pricking in her two eyes. But when she saw the longed-for thing, it was then her tears came freely. With her right arm she hugged her child and with her left she hugged the skin. Then she called her two sons and kissed them and then she kissed her babe again. After that she set her face seaward, pulled on her skin, dived in the water and was gone.

And that was the last time they saw her. Except that once on a warm and lingering night when their father took them out in the boat and the moon was low and full and glowing, a grey-eyed silky seal came by and kept pace with the boat for many a mile, but when they turned for home, it dipped down and vanished beneath the water never to be seen again.

20
The Tale of Thomas the Rhymer

The Third Harper came forward and, lifting up his plain oak harp, laid it on his knee and played three strong chords on its lower strings. His unkempt sandy hair fell into his eyes and strayed over his dark green cloak. His tan boots were worn with walking and his young face was lined, but the hands that woke the strings on his beloved instrument were lithe and agile. With a glance at the First Harper, he put his harp down and addressed the crowd:

Like the Ballad of Tam Lin, my tale is also of a faerie queen who lures a young man to the Otherworld. Yet my tale is different. For, although the faerie queen is just as beautiful and alluring, she is not completely wicked, and has a care for the young man's soul. Because of this, she only allows him one binding to the Land of Faerie and prevents the other two, as you shall see. And my tale is not just a warning of the dangers of that land, for hidden within it is a map to guide the traveller there in safety. For, though it is rash indeed to make such a journey, there are riches to be discovered in that land, riches of the soul. But the price of the journey is high, and the traveller who returns will afterwards be caught between two worlds.

So, as I tell the tale, take heed of the three bindings which would keep Thomas in the Otherworld, and watch out for the places that he goes to on his journey. For the grassy bank is a gateway to the Otherworld, the garden of enchanted fruit is a snare to the soul, and the choosing of the ways must be made by all travellers. Remember, too, that the barrier of blood and water is the final border of the realm of Faerie.

Then the harper knelt and played a strong and rousing melody on his harp, so that its low rich tones ran round the cave. Keeping the harp near so that he could decorate the story with little flourishes, he began his tale:

Thomas was a poet and already had a little of the Knowing before this adventure fell to him. It was on a fair morning when he was lying on a bank of the River Huntlie with his harp beside him. The tune he had made on it was in his head and he was fitting the words to it when out of the corner of his eye he saw a flash of green. He moved his head and saw it again. Squinting against the sun he saw a figure on horseback. It was a woman dressed in a green silk tunic which sparkled as she moved. Thomas stood up and scrabbled for his cap. His face reddened at the sight and beauty of the woman and he bowed to her.

'Hail, Queen of Heaven,' he said.

'No, no!' she laughed and the myriad silver bells on the horse's bridle chirruped and tinkled along with her, 'I am no Queen of Heaven, but the Queen of Elfland. But you may come with me now and bring your harp and I will take you there.' She paused and laughed again, 'Though only', says she, 'if you will dare to kiss me on the lips.'

And when brave Thomas heard these words
for good or bad as it may be
he upped and kissed her full and hard
and thus he touched the great faerie.

'And now', she said, 'that you've touched my lips
it's your body that you have bound to me
and you must serve me for seven whole years
through weal or woe, as the case may be.'

And that was the first binding to Faeryland.

After that Thomas jumped onto the white horse and rode behind her. Urged by the ringing bridle, the horse sped faster than the wind. They rode across valley, moorland and desert. On and on they travelled, crossing wild country and wading across rivers until darkness fell.

Then they came to a river that ran red with blood. They waded through this also and at once the landscape changed and Thomas found himself in a rare, fair garden filled with fruit trees.

'Lady,' said Thomas, 'let us dismount here so that I can pull down some of the fruit for us to eat.'

Forbear, True Thomas, cried the queen,
to touch the fruit upon the tree
for all the plagues that lurk in hell
lie in the fruit of this country.

And that was the second binding, but Thomas had warning of it.

Seeing he was hungry the queen took out a bottle of wine and a loaf of bread and gave him some. Then she led him to the top of a hill and showed him a place where three roads met.

'There,' she says, 'can you make out a narrow path, half-covered in brambles?'

'I can,' says Thomas.

'That is the path of holiness. Few find it, and of those who find it few remain on it. But do you also see the wide and grassy one that runs through flowery meadows?'

'I can', says he.

'Well, that is the broad path to wickedness that is trodden by many. But look again, Thomas, and you will see a third path half-hidden, which winds its way to the Land of Faerie. That is our path. But first I must charge you to hold your tongue after we get there.

> For if you speak but e'en one word
> in all the time you spend with me
> you ne'er will see your own homeland
> or mortal kind before you die.

And that was the third binding. But Thomas heeded the warning of the queen for he spoke not one word in the land of Faerie in all the time he was there.

The queen clothed him in an elfin coat and green velvet shoes and he served her for seven years. But years run swiftly in the land of Faerie and it seemed that only a short time had passed when the queen told him he must return to Ercildoune. She said that if he stayed for more than seven years, his soul might be taken as a tithe to Hell.

'Make yourself ready, Thomas,' says she, 'and I will take you back to your home and people.'

As they prepared to leave, the queen went to an apple tree and pulled a fruit from it.

'Here,' she said, 'take this as your wage. It will give you the gift of truth-telling and prophecy and, besides that, it will make you rich.'

After he returned to the mortal world, Thomas was changed. He had a strangeness about him that made men wary of him. Added to this, he had kept hold of the apple and once he was safely home he ate it. Now he was unable to do other than speak the blunt truth to everyone he met, good or bad. At the same time he felt the power of the seer come on him, and it was not long before he earned a reputation for his prophecies and many came to consult him. Then he would look into the future and perhaps warn or admonish them or teach them patience or give them hope as the need and the truth might be - and in this way he did indeed become rich. He also took a wife, and though he loved her well, she began to grow old as mortals do, and Thomas still had the tail ribbon of his heart tied to the Faerie Queen whom he had once served body and soul.

Then a day came when his wife returned home and told him of a strange thing. She said that a pure white doe had come into the woods and could not be moved by man or dog. Then Thomas rose up and, taking his harp, went into the woods and came up to the white creature. But what he said to her and where he went cannot be known. For from that time onwards he was never seen again on this earth.

21
The Love Story of Diarmaid and Grainne

After the three bards had told their tales, the people made their choices and cast their votes. And, though the bards had seemed equal in skill, because the listeners were surrounded by the sea and already half in love with the fantastic and beautiful creatures that lived in its waters, they gave the prize to the Second Harper for her tale of the Sea Maiden.

Now it was the custom that the bard who received the prize should tell a great tale and that the tale should be one of heroism, love, passion and mystery, such as would fill the hearts of all who listened. Often the story was already known to them, but the bard was expected to bring new thoughts and awakenings by adding to it poems and music to draw out its wonders. In this way, the crowd hoped to receive entertainment from sundown to sunrise, for that was how long the tale should last.

As soon as the Second Harper had received her silver cup, the people rose and went to walk about the island and find refreshment. Then, as dusk descended, they gathered again in the mouth of the great cave and stilled themselves to hear the story of the night.

The other two bards were already in their seats, waiting for the woman harper to come into the cave. When she entered, the people saw that she wore a long dress of blue silk with a dark red cloak thrown over it, clasped with a silver brooch. She bowed to them and sat down beside her jewelled harp.

'The tale that I shall tell you', she said, 'comes from Erin, although many believe it belongs to Alba as well. But as the story is long and has many parts, I would like help in the telling of it. So I have asked the First Harper to tell us about Diarmaid who was a member of the war-band, the Fianna, for such prowess is his passion. And, at the same time, we shall hear about Finn mac Cumhail, the Captain of that band, for without him none of this would have happened. Indeed, he is rather like the ogre in the tale who, in seeking to guard his youthful treasure, threatens instead to withhold its quickening power.'

Then the woman smiled at the First Harper and sat back on her rush-covered seat.

The bard with the black beard came forward and bowed. He thanked the woman and addressed the crowd:

'There is an early story that concerns this love-tale,' he said, 'and as it is one of violence and revenge, it seems right that I should tell it.'

He smiled.

'But first I should like you to know of the Fianna, the war-band led by Finn. For there was no band in the land to equal it. It was seven battalions' strong by the time of this tale, and every man of it had undergone such tests as beggar belief! And when I tell you that Diarmaid O'Dyna was the most skilled and daring man among them, you will perhaps understand why his loss was so great to Finn and why his treachery rankled in the great leader's heart.

But what will astonish you most is this – no warrior could be armed with weapons until he was first armed with the power of the Word. Every man of the Fianna had first to memorize the Twelve Books of Poetry and learn to compose verse – a bardic training indeed! Only after mastering such poetic art could he attempt the high tests of prowess. And, as to these, if you want to know how difficult *they* were, I shall tell you now!

Leaning over his proud harp, the bard began playing a lively jig upon it, after which he sang these verses, jauntily fitting them to the rhythms of the tune:

> First the Fenian warrior must,
> while buried to his knees in earth,
> with shield and hazel stick ward off
> the thrust of nine great hurtling spears –
> must parry nine great spears at once
> by nine strong warriors bravely thrown
> from nine-ridge distance of the land
> and suffer not one wounding!
>
> Then he must bind his hair in braids
> and, with a single tree-length's start,
> must run within a wood, pursued
> by Fenian warriors close behind.
> But if a single braid be loosed,
> or one stick crack beneath his feet,
> or if he tangles with one branch,
> or if his weapons shake, he fails!

And last, the would-be warrior must,
while running through the woods once more,
leap high, and nimbly soar above
a lath held level with his brow.
Then he must, running, stoop beneath
a lath held level with his knee
and draw a thorn from out his foot
but never must he slacken speed! ⑯

'And even if he passes all these tests,' said the bard as he finished the jig, 'he must swear allegiance to the band and forsake all family and tribal bonds. He must courteously accept all offers of hospitality, must never turn his back on battle, always honour women and, if he should marry, refuse to take a dowry.'

Sweeping back his fine cloak, he announced in a voice breaking with emotion:

Well was it claimed by such great heroes:
'Truth was in our hearts and strength within our arms
and those things that we promised, we fulfilled.'

Wiping a tear from his eye, he continued:

Diarmaid passed all these tests and was the most fleet-footed among the Fianna. He also developed a special skill with his spears so that he was able to leap high over any obstacle. But, though he became famous for his prowess, his fierce daring first came to him when he was a boy and was drawn from the power of a wild boar, with whom his fate was bound up. And if you want to know how this pairing of Diarmaid and the magical beast – who was both weal and woe to him, came about, I shall tell you the story of it now:

When Diarmaid was a small boy he was sent for fostering to Aengus Og, the god of love, and was brought up in his magical palace known as the *Brugh* beside the river Boyne. Aengus' court was one of the most revered and favoured places in the whole of Ireland in those days. The god had many foster-children and there were many visitors coming and going in that great palace. Though her husband lived elsewhere, Diarmaid's mother lived mostly with her son at the Brugh. But while she was there she was unfaithful and gave herself to Roc, Aengus' steward, and afterwards bore him a child. When her husband discovered that the second child was not his own, pain and jealousy began to rankle in him.

As he said this, the harper struck the harp-strings with the back of his nails making a sound that was harsh and discordant. The cacophany came back to him from every jagged rock-edge within the cave and in a loud voice he declaimed above the noise:

As the years passed, his dark passion grew. Whenever he visited the palace on the Boyne he saw the looks that passed between his wife and Roc and was certain that they still loved one another, but he kept his thoughts to himself. Then one day, when he was playing with Diarmaid, the servant's son ran between his legs to escape some fighting hounds. In a sudden fit of hatred and jealousy, Diarmaid's father caught him and squeezed him between his knees until the breath left him, then he threw him to the floor. Hearing the boy's anguished cries, Roc rushed in and, holding his dying son in his arms, snatched up a druidic wand and summoned a shapechanging spell on the boy, at the same time uttering a curse on Diarmaid.

The harper lowered his voice until it was almost a growl. Slithering his nails back and forth across the lower strings of the harp, he said:

And the shapechange and the curse was this, that the child would become a wild boar and would live on the slopes of Ben Bulben, the great mountain in the north of Ireland and would hold in his heart a name, a smell and a vengeance until the time came. And the second part of it was this, that once he was a grown man and a warrior, Diarmaid would meet his death by a bristle of the boar.

Then the man sealed this utterance with words and signs of power after which his son's body thickened and grew spikes of black hair, his head shrunk into his shoulders, his face sprouted tusks and his legs shortened, splaying out from his body. Then, earless and tail-less, the creature ran shrieking from the hall and out into the wild, and none dared follow it.

After his voice had died away, the harper continued striking his harp with the harsh nail tones for some time before plucking the strings with his finger-ends again. When he had brought us into a softer place, he smiled at the Second Harper and, with a final flourish, put his harp aside.

With his last notes still humming behind her in the cave, the Second Harper stepped forward and thanked him, and while the First Harper bowed low and the sound of clapping echoed among the rocks, she pushed back her long hair so that the crowd could see again her pale and lovely face. When all fell quiet once more, she said:

Besides the power of curse, the terrible power of Love itself runs through this story. It begins with Aengus Og, the god of love, who fostered Diarmaid. But it is also in the *Ball Seirc*, the Love-spot on Diarmaid's brow. For those of you who do not know how he came by it, the story is curious and takes place a little time before the fateful meeting of the lovers. And, because it concerns a woman from the Otherworld, I have asked the Third Harper to tell it to us.

As she spoke, the Third Harper rose from his seat and came into the middle of the cave. He bent over his stout and simple harp and drew from it a lilting air, which he decorated with many fine cuts and grace-notes. When he came to the last chord he kept his fingers shimmering on the strings so that its haunting modal harmonies went rippling round the cave. Then he, too, spoke above its music:

After Diarmaid had been a warrior with the Fianna for several years, he and three of his companions were out hunting in the forest. They hunted all day and by evening were very weary, for they had not caught their prey and darkness was closing on them. They saw an old hut in the middle of the wood and decided to ask whoever lived there if they might have shelter for the night. They went up to it and knocked on the wooden door. After a while they heard someone fumbling at the other side, and soon the door was opened by a wizened old man who beckoned them inside.

They went in and found themselves in a small parlour. A young girl was sitting beside the fire. She started when they entered and turned on them a face of such beauty that the men could only stare in astonishment at her. It seemed to them that the radiance of the sunlight itself shone from her. Her eyes were blue as the hyacinth and her skin white as the snowdrop in early spring. When she moved her head splinters of gold flashed and glinted in her long hair. The three men could hardly take their eyes from her and it was with a great effort that they finally turned their attention to the old man while the girl went to make supper.

But as they sat down to eat, an old sheep that had been sitting quietly beside the wall, suddenly leaped up and landed on the table. The plates and cups fell jangling together and the wine spilled onto the floor. Immediately all three warriors jumped up and tried to wrestle the sheep off the table, but each found to his great embarrassment that he was unable to move it. They struggled with it a second time, and the three of them even pitted their strength and tried to move it together, but despite all their efforts the sheep still lay sprawled in front of them and teased them with its loud bleating.

After they finally admitted defeat, the old man called to a black cat who was sitting in the hearth. As soon as it heard the call, the cat jumped up onto the table and, taking the sheep's collar in its mouth, led it away easily. Seeing this the warriors became very angry and demanded an explanation. The old man held up his hand to calm them: 'It is quite simple,' he said, 'for the old bellwether that just now you were unable to wrestle to the floor

– is the World. And the black cat that I called just now is Death, for it is only Death that can overcome the World.'

And he would have said more, but the maiden put a finger to her lips and the old man sank back into his chair and closed his eyes.

The men fell quiet then, pondering on these mysteries until the fire died down and preparations were made for the night. The old man showed them to a chamber at the back of the hut where they made ready for bed. But as soon as they lay down, the door opened and in came the maiden carrying a candle. She went to one of the men and bent over him, lifting up her candle so that it shone on his face. He tried to draw her into his bed, but she refused his advances. She went to the second man and he, too, tried to make her lie down with him, but she refused him also. Lastly she came to Diarmaid and when he reached for her, she said to him: 'You may not have me Diarmaid, for though I once belonged to you I can never be yours again.'

As she spoke these words the maiden drew herself up and the scent of honeysuckle and hawthorn filled the room. The men stared in astonishment as her beautiful white skin began to glow with light. They saw that her veins were delicate as young leaves and her skin glistened as if bathed with dew. She tossed her head and her golden hair fell glinting around her shoulders. Then she smiled and said in a voice as sweet as birdsong: 'I am Youth.'

She turned to Diarmaid and said: 'Though you may no longer possess me I will give you something to make all women who look upon you love you.'

With that she pressed her finger to his brow and when she took it back again, there was the love-mark, the *Ball Seirc,* glowing on his skin, and pulsing with the mysterious energy of love.

The harper paused and smiled.

'And after that time', he said, 'wherever he went, Diarmaid drew upon him the desire of women.'

He put aside his harp.

'I know what you men are thinking,' he said. 'Each one of you is wishing that you were also marked with the Ball Seirc. You are thinking what a fine thing it would be to command the love of women. And so did Diarmaid at first. But so strong was the effect of the mark that he was forever having to soothe and placate all the plain women who had fallen victim to him. So, at last he was driven to wear a cap pulled down over his brow to give him some peace, for he decided that, in the matter of love, he would prefer after all to choose and not be chosen.'

Looking round at the crowd again, the harper said: 'But such choices are not made by mortals. They are the gift of the gods.'

Then he bowed and, as the cave filled again with the sound of clapping, went and sat to one side of the Second Harper. She bent towards him and whispered something in his ear at which he nodded. After that she stood up and came forward into the middle of the cave.

'And now,' she said, 'you know of the Fianna and of their prowess and you know of Finn, their leader, who carries a passion within him that wars with his age and wisdom. And you also know of Diarmaid, of the curse that waits for him and the Love-spot that is on him. But you do not yet know of the Princess Grainne. Though, perhaps some of you have heard of her father Cormac mac Art, the High King of Ireland. But now the time has come to tell you one of the greatest love-stories in the world. Listen as I begin the tale, for you will meet Grainne within it soon enough.'

Then she struck a light, tinkling chord on her little harp and began:

Now the great Finn Mac Cumhail, Captain of the Fianna – brave warrior that he was and blessed with the power of Otherworldly Seeing, was in need of companionship. Oisin, his son, and Dering, his Druid, saw him early one morning pacing the green sward outside his palace in grief and loneliness. They went to him and asked what was the matter.

'I have been unable to sleep ever since my wife died,' he replied. 'I miss her sorely and there is no one to take her place.'

'Then we shall search the length and breadth of Ireland and find you the fairest and most deserving woman there is,' said Oisin. 'In that way you will find love again.'

Finn was heartened by their concern and sent them on this quest with his blessing.

As soon as they were on their way, Dering told Oisin that he already had a woman in mind.

'She is a perfect choice,' he said, 'young and beautiful, high-born and gifted with druidic knowledge.'

'Then why did you not tell Finn about her?' asked Oisin.

'Because she is the daughter of the High King, Cormac mac Art, and he and Finn once quarrelled long ago and to this day have not made peace with one another.'

'Then let us ask on his behalf and see how we fare,' said Oisin.

So the two men journeyed to Tara and before long reached the High King's Court. They were welcomed with great courtesy and brought before the King.

'Lord,' they said, bowing low, 'we have come from Finn Mac

Cumhaill, captain of the Fianna. He is looking for a new wife and we have been sent to ask you for the hand of your daughter, Grainne.'

Cormac mac Art rose to his feet in the great hall with the flashing shields hanging from the walls and his costly jewelled cloak across his shoulders. He fixed them with his eyes and they quailed before him, expecting a rebuke. Instead he said, 'You would be very fortunate if she agrees to marry Finn for she has so far refused every offer from every suitor that has come her way. Nevertheless, I will ask her for you.'

And with that he turned and made his way to his daughter's chamber.

Grainne was in her chamber lying on her couch. She was wearing a long green tunic and her fair hair was tumbled about her on the bedding. Her books tossed aside, she lay on her back gazing into the air as if seeing a vision. And so she was, for her mind was in the Otherworld. She was remembering how as a child she had been taken there by a tall man in a long cloak of many colours that shimmered and glittered as he walked. He had carried a silver branch with golden bells on it and she had followed this sound as if compelled by a strange magic. He took her through the mist into another land where she had found her mother and brother already waiting for her. Together they had seen many wonders, beautiful palaces, elegant courtyards, houses with roofs thatched with bird-feathers, and they had discovered magic cups and wands and cauldrons and heard much tale-telling. But the greatest wonder of all was the dark and secret well, which lay half-hidden under a circle of hazel trees.

Never could she forget the well, for, though it was small and hidden, deep in its mirroring bowl darted small fish like silver streaks while below them lurked mysterious speckled salmon. She remembered the lure of its sparkling waters and she remembered the moment when she filled the bronze cup with its pure liquid and held it to her lips. But most of all she remembered what happened after she had drunk from it. For in that instant a veil was lifted and she could see the seamlessness of everything that had ever been, everything that was and everything that was waiting to be, dark and light, life and death, joy and woe. She now knew that everything was joined by threads of light, and that nothing stood alone.

But she had not been long in the Otherworld before her father came to take them back to Tara. Nevertheless while he was there he, too, drank from the Well of Wisdom. And, though they rarely spoke of their experience, Grainne knew that they were both changed forever because of it.

The bard's voice had become almost a whisper. She stopped speaking and stretched out her arm for her slender harp. Lifting it towards her she drew a delicate filigree of sound from the strings. She played softly while the truths of her words flowed round the cave and into the hearts of the listeners:

Rich and rare were the gems she wore
And a bright gold ring on her finger she bore
But O, her beauty was far beyond
Her sparkling gems, her snow-white hand.

When I was a child I was stolen away

By Manannan mac Lir, god of the sea.
He took me to the island of *Tír na n'Og*,
A magical land where none grows old.

Rich and rare were the gems she wore
And a bright gold ring on her finger she bore
But O, her beauty was far beyond
Her sparkling gems, her snow-white hand.

A land of feasting, a land of song
Where only the brave and the fair belong,
Where the salmon leaps and the hazel tree grows
And the Fountain of Wisdom ever flows.

Rich and rare were the gems she wore
And a bright gold ring on her finger she bore
But O, her beauty was far beyond
Her sparkling gems, her snow-white hand.

I drank of the Waters of Wisdom and then
My father the King carried me home.
And now I have beauty and wit besides,
And the Goddess herself looks out of my eyes. ⑰

Breathing the name of Grainne into the hollows of the cave, the harper put her harp aside and continued with the story:

When King Cormac entered his daughter's chamber, he saw the faraway look in her eyes and knew at once that her mind was in the Otherworld. He bent and kissed her cheek to try and break her from her reverie and said: 'Grainne, I have some men here from Finn Mac Cumhail. He has sent to ask if you will be his wife. What do you say?'

The girl's thoughts turned at once to the deeds of warriors, their hunts, their quests, their prowess and their conquests. She remembered being told once that Finn had a head of beautiful yellow hair, that he was invincible in battle and that he had the faerie power of far-sighted vision in his thumb. All these things swelled her mind and she answered in a voice of one in a dream: 'If it pleases you, father, why should it not please me.'

Cormac returned to the men and told them that Grainne had agreed to the betrothal. But after he had left her chamber, Grainne went back to her reverie in the Otherworld and forgot about her rash reply.

Thus it was that two weeks later she was surprised to find her father entertaining Finn and the Fianna to a grand feast. She was even more surprised to find she was put in the place of honour next to Finn. She asked Dara, her father's druid: 'Why is Finn here?'

'Surely you know that this is your betrothal feast?'

Grainne was shocked, for the young Finn with the golden locks was long gone. Now Finn's beard was white, his hair grey and his skin wrinkled and hoary. A thrill of fear ran through her heart while she looked along the line of men sitting on either side of him. There was his son Oisin, stately and youthful with his black doe-eyes and, beside him, his grandson Oscar with a mane of yellow hair. 'Even he would not be too young,' she thought. Her eye was still travelling round the company when it suddenly fell on Diarmaid. His face was in shadow for he wore a cap pulled down low over his brow, but stray locks of his wild black hair escaped from it and fell prettily upon his cheeks, or so it seemed to Grainne.

Just then there came a sharp noise of dogs barking and in burst some of Finn's hounds snapping and snarling at each other. Diarmaid jumped up and went among them, soothing and petting them until they quietened. Grainne watched as he bent over them and pushed up his cap. He turned and caught her looking at him and pulled the cap down at once, but it was too late, for in that moment Grainne had caught a glimpse of the *Ball Seirc*, the love-mark on his brow. At sight of it a fierce energy seemed to burn into her heart. She reached for her goblet and took a deep draught of wine to steady the violent trembling that had suddenly come upon her. At the same time she heard the imperious voice of Finn calling her name, and next moment he began speaking to her in the Druid's riddling tongue. With a great effort she composed herself, commanding the Secret Knowledge to rise in her and meet his challenge.

'Tell me,' said Finn, smiling and leaning towards her, 'What is more plentiful than the blades of grass?'

Grainne returned his gaze coolly:

'The dew, for a single blade holds many drops,' she replied.

'And what vessel holds any cargo?' asked Finn.

'A blacksmith's tongs,' she answered, 'holding both hot and cold.'

'What has no lock or chain to bind it?' he asked.

'The eye of a man who watches his friend.'

Finn nodded, but his keen eyes still bored into hers.

'What is the best jewel?' he asked.

'A sharp knife.'

'What is the best food?'

'Milk,' said Grainne, flashing her white teeth, 'for it feeds both children and old men.'

There was a pause in which one of the Fenians gave a short laugh and then fell silent.

Finn sat back in his chair and put his finger-tips together:

'What is the greatest of deeds?'

'One of high honour with no arrogance,' said Grainne.

'And what is more brittle than a sow's thistle?' asked Finn, raising one of his great shaggy eyebrows.

Grainne looked round the whole company who were now paying full attention. She said: 'The questions of an old wild boar.'

At this there was a roar of laughter from the men.

Finn frowned and leaned closer.

'And what is hotter than fire?' he asked.

'A woman's choosing between two men,' she replied, stealing a glance at Diarmaid.

'And what is swifter than the wind?'

'A woman's thought,' she said, 'between two men.'

'What is sharper than a sword?' said Finn, and his voice was edged.

'The reproach of your enemy.'

'And what is softer than swan's down?' he said in a voice soft as silk.

'The touch of a lover's palm upon my cheek,' replied Grainne, glancing again at Diarmaid, while a faint blush rose in her face.

'And what,' said Finn, sitting back again, 'is whiter than snow?'

'The truth,' said Grainne, and her words rang out in the silence.

'And what is blacker than a raven?'

'Death,' she whispered.

At this Finn raised his glass and toasted Grainne to indicate that he was satisfied. But Grainne drank her wine in silence and looked again at Diarmaid. Then, offering to fetch more wine, she slipped from her place and lifted down a heavy flagon. She dropped a sleeping herb into it and took it round the company, serving all at the table except Oisin, Oscar and Diarmaid.

Soon the sound of heavy breathing filled the dining hall as one by one the older warriors succumbed to the herb and their heads dropped forward onto the table. As soon as she was sure they were deeply asleep Grainne went up to Oisin. Putting her arm on his shoulder, she looked him in the eyes and asked him if he would elope with her. Oisin gazed at her in astonishment, disturbed and flustered by her close presence and the question she asked him. When at last words came to him, with a glance at the hoary head of Finn collapsed on the table nearby, he muttered reluctantly: 'Madam, I may not.'

Undaunted, Grainne went to Oscar and asked him the same question but he, too, slid his eyes away from her and, looking at Finn, dejectedly muttered that he was unable to go with her. Then she went to Diarmaid and looked into his beautiful grey eyes while her face flushed and went pale by turns.

'Will *you* go with me, Diarmaid?' she asked.

Diarmaid averted his gaze and said quietly: 'My loyalty is also with Finn.'

Grainne drew herself up. 'Then I will put a *geis* on you,' she said.

Diarmaid looked at her. 'That is an evil thing you ask of me and I beg you to leave such thinking,' he replied.

She said in a low trembling voice: 'Tell me truly, Diarmaid, do I not stir desire within your heart.'

Diarmaid answered: 'I will not go with you. You must not ask this of me.'

Then he sprang up and cried out in a voice so loud it echoed round the hall and threatened to wake the sleeping warriors:

'Grainne! I swear I will take you neither in softness nor hardness, nor without nor within, nor on horseback nor on foot.' So saying, he strode down the length of the hall and went outside and shut himself in his lodging.

Grainne watched him go and then ran to her own chamber and threw herself down on the bed. Her heart weighed heavy with the love that swelled within her. She thought of the man she had unwittingly pledged to marry and of the man who had thrown enchantment over her. At last she began to sob as she thought of everything that she had once enjoyed, everything that had once given her gladness and that now seemed to have lost all meaning for her.

The bard broke from the tale and said: 'Because I am a woman and feel such things keenly, I have composed a poem of love to Diarmaid showing the nature of his beauty, a poem such as Grainne might herself have written.' Then, drawing from her harp a plaintive and insistent rhythm, she began to half-sing, half-speak this refrain:

And after setting eyes on Diarmaid,

afterwards she said:
There is nothing more beautiful to me now,
not the berries on the mountain ash –
the bright red berries against the snow,
unless it is his red lips in his face so white.
Nor yet the blue-black gleaming feathers of the crow
unless it is his blue-black hair upon his brow.
Nor yet the sight of a young willow-tree in bud
unless it is his smooth white body without fault –
the limbs so straight and slender and the eyes grey as a dove,
the face so shapely, narrow below and broad above.
And thus, when she thought of Diarmaid,
so she thought of love,
For he, touched by the faerie love-spot was so white and fair
that no man born of woman might with him compare.

(18)

And because in her music she tempered the grief-strain with the sleep-strain, all who listened were quietened as if by a subtle magic.

'And now,' she said, putting aside her harp, 'having felt her grief, let us see how Grainne fares, for do not forget that she has the power, the wit and the wisdom of the Otherworld:

When she had wept and consoled herself and wept again, Grainne remembered the *geis* she had begun to put on Diarmaid and the words that he had put on her in return. Then she thought of her own druidic powers, and of the cry of her heart that must be answered. A plan came to her then, and she quickly dressed herself in fresh clothes and went out.

Diarmaid was still in his lodging and had refused all comers. He was cursing the fact that his love-spot was such a burden to him. Usually it attracted the love of women for whom he felt nothing. This time, however, it had drawn the High King's daughter, a woman so astonishingly clever and beautiful that she would be a prize for any man. Yet to have her love was to forswear his lord and captain. He was still wrestling with these thoughts when there came a strange scuffling outside his door after which he heard Grainne's voice calling to him: 'Are you inside, Diarmaid, and will you not come out and escape with me now.'

Diarmaid raised himself up and spoke roughly because of his torment: 'Have I not sworn an oath to you, woman!' he shouted angrily.

He waited for a retort from her, but when she made no answer, he got up and unlatched the door. He pushed it open and was surprised when it came back in his face. He pushed it again as far as he could and peered round. He saw that Grainne was sitting on a buck goat and that it was jammed between the two sides of his doorway.

'Now,' she said triumphantly, 'I am neither within nor without, nor am I on foot nor on a horse!'

As Diarmaid gave no answer, she dismounted and pulled the goat into the courtyard, saying to him: 'I have such love for you, Diarmaid, that I am placing this *geis* on you, which is one of the spells at my command. I would have laid it on you in the great hall but you refused me, and now I have broken your words of refusal. So I am again binding you with this *geis* to take me away, for besides loving you with my whole heart, I will not abide marriage to an old man.'

As soon as she had spoken, she raised her slender white arms and began to sing in a soft, hypnotic voice:

'I adjure you by the nine green-necked waves of the sea
by the powers of the air beaten with the wings of birds,
by the power of the fire that burnishes the bright sword,
by the powers of the earth that shield the dwellings of the *sidhe*.
By these powers I conjure you, Diarmaid, to save me from Finn.'

Then she lowered her arms and came closer to him still singing in a strange, compelling voice:

'For am I not fair as the best enchantress?
Am I not beautiful as the jewelled moon?
Do I not hold in my hand the gold cup of song
And do I not carry within me the night-dark mysteries of woman?'

As she sang she came so close that he could feel her breath on his face. Then she murmured in a low, melodious voice: 'Tell me truly, Diarmaid, do I not wake within your heart the seed-bright stirrings of love?'

The power of her spell was very great, but Diarmaid kept his eyes lowered so as not to meet her gaze and fall beneath it. He answered in a cold and courteous tone:

'Lady, whatever spells you lay on me, as you know full well, Finn has been given the keys to the palace as is the custom, so we cannot escape.'

Her eyes flashing, Grainne answered: 'There is a wicket gate from my chamber. We can leave through that.'

'But I am under *geis* never to pass through such a gate,' said Diarmaid.

'Then run at it with your spear and vault over it, for I know you have this skill,' she replied.

At this, Diarmaid spread his hands in despair and went into the dining hall to find his companions. He saw the older members of the Fianna still sleeping, and Finn among them, but the younger ones had gone. With a heavy heart he went in search of Oisin and Oscar. He found them in their lodging and asked them what he should do. They looked at him with a mixture of pity and envy and said that though they feared for his safety, nevertheless he was now bound by Grainne's *geis* and had no choice but to go with her. Then the three men wept and embraced each other for they knew that Diarmaid's days with the Fianna were over.

Late that night the couple left the palace, he by vaulting over the main gate, and she by slipping through the wicket gate. For a while they made swift progress under cover of night until Grainne suddenly threw herself on the ground and declared that she was too weary to go any further.

'Then let us return before it is too late,' said Diarmaid.'

'No,' she answered,' for I know where we can find a chariot and horses.'

Grainne took him to a stout-fenced meadow where they found a chariot with two horses. They yoked both horses to it and travelled swiftly towards the Ford of Luan on the River Shannon.

The harper raised her head and her eyes swept round the crowd.

'And there we will leave them for a while,' she said, 'except to say that, though Diarmaid went with Grainne, he kept his heart to himself, for he was not yet ready to accept his fate.'

The people stirred as if waking from a dream. Beginning to murmur to each other, they opened their bundles and took out the food they had prepared. Some had cold chops, some had flat trenchers of bread with slices of cold pork across them, others had fruit and cheeses. Many of them shared their food and handed round their wine. Soon the cave was filled with the clinking of cups and goblets and the buzz of conversation. Some compared the telling with the stories of other years and some bragged about their own prowess on the harp. As the wine flowed, all agreed that the woman told her tale prettily enough and that the night was as good as expected.

When they had finished eating, they sat down again and waited for the harper to continue. There was silence as she came back into the cave, her red cloak glowing in the candle-light. Kneeling to her harp, she let loose a handful of silvery notes and, raising her voice, began to speak:

Next morning Finn awoke in the Great Hall of the palace, to find his bride gone and Diarmaid with her. Raging like a wild boar, he went about the court shouting at his men, and ordering them to arm themselves. Although still stiff after their drugged sleep, the older warriors began to make themselves ready, but the younger ones were reluctant to go after their companion. They tried to remonstrate with Finn but he refused to listen to them. So, at his insistence, they armed themselves and, mustering the horses, set out in pursuit of the lovers.

Meanwhile Diarmaid and Grainne had crossed the River Shannon and hidden themselves in a small forest known as 'The Wood of the Two Tents'. Grainne was tired and said she needed a place to rest so Diarmaid built a hut out of branches to shelter them. They thought they were well ahead of Finn, but Finn had already sent two fast runners to seek them out. The men came to the wood and one of them climbed into the branches of a tree. He looked down and, scanning the wood, saw the hut with Diarmaid and Grainne inside it. But he also saw that Diarmaid had protected the hut with a strong fence containing seven doors. The two men returned to Finn and told him what they had seen. As soon as he heard where the couple were hiding, he gave orders to his men to go in that direction. Again the Fianna, reluctant to fight with their companion, did their best to dissuade him. But Finn would have none of it and marched on towards the wood. When they reached the hut where Diarmaid and Grainne were hiding, he posted a company of his men outside each of the seven doors.

As the warriors waited by the doors, far away in his palace beside the Boyne, Aengus Og, the love god, felt a great pain in his breast. He knew at once that it was Diarmaid calling on his heart, for Diarmaid was to Aengus as his own soul. Immediately, the young god opened his great wings and flew with the speed of the wind to where Diarmaid and Grainne were imprisoned. He hovered above the hut and dropped silently through the air hidden from view by the *faed feea*, his cloak of invisibility. Appearing suddenly before the couple he said to them: 'Wrap this round you quickly, and let me carry you to safety!' and he held out the cloak.

Diarmaid told him he would be ashamed to escape so easily.

'But take Grainne,' he said, 'and keep her with you until I come.'

So Aengus lifted Grainne in his arms and, wrapping her in the *faed feea*, spread his great wings and rose into the air with her.

As soon as they were gone, Diarmaid went to the first of the seven doors and called to the men outside, asking who they were.

'Oisin and Oscar and the Clan Baskin,' they replied. 'We are not enemies to you. Come out and we will protect you.'

But Diarmaid refused their help. Then he went to the second door and asked who was there.

'Cailte Mac Ronan and the Clan Ronan,' came the answer. 'Come out at this gate and we will defend you against Finn.

But again Diarmaid refused. After that he went to each of the doors and at each found friendship and protection, but at the sixth stood a clan who hated him and at the seventh, stood Finn himself.

Then Diarmaid called out boldly: 'This is the door I will pass through, O Finn!' And, taking his two spears, he launched himself into the air and leaped high over the fence and over the men's heads, landing far beyond them. Swift as the wind he ran until he reached the Wood of Two Sallows where Aengus had taken Grainne.

The couple stayed there under Aengus' protection until the god said that it was time for him to leave. Then he reminded them of the power that was in Finn's thumb. For Finn had once caught it in the door of a faerie mound and ever afterwards when he put it in his mouth his sight travelled far beyond mortal range and he could see with his inner eye whatever he wished. So, before he left them, the god charged them with these warnings: never to hide in a tree with one trunk, never to shelter in a cave with one entrance, never to trust to an island with one mooring-site, never to eat food in the place where they cooked it, never to sleep where they had eaten, and never to spend two nights in the same place.

But as they continued their flight, Diarmaid was even wilier than this. To outwit the power of Finn's thumb, he took bracken from the woods and laid it beside them when they were sleeping on the shore, and he took sand and laid it beneath them when they slept in the woods. Thus, when Finn put his thumb in his mouth and saw in his mind's eye the places where they lay, he was tricked as to their whereabouts. For, when he pursued them to the sea shore, they laughed their way through the woods and when he pursued them in the woods, they ran freely along the shore. In this way, the couple were able to keep several days ahead of him.

Nevertheless, knowing that Finn would eventually find the places where they had rested, Diarmaid decided to leave signs for him, such as a piece of unbroken bread or an uneaten fish. He was careful not to let Grainne know of these signs, for in them lay a message for Finn that Grainne was still a maid.

But, as the days went by and Diarmaid made no move towards her, Grainne began to feel insulted. So, one day when they were crossing a swollen stream and the water splashed up to her waist, she called out in derision: 'See Diarmaid, how bold the water is, for it dares to touch me where you dare not. And you a captain of the Fianna!'

As Grainne laughed scornfully at him, Diarmaid's face

reddened first with shame and afterwards with anger. He strode towards her, lifted her up and laid her down on the bank. Then, tearing off her wet tunic, he took her there and then in the mud and the bracken beside the river.

Afterwards, knowing that his fate with Grainne was sealed and that he would never return to the Fianna, Diarmaid began to cast about in his mind for a safe place to take her where they might live in peace. He was puzzling over this next day when a thought came to him.

'Grainne,' he said, 'have you heard of the Forest of Dooros?'

'Of course!' she replied, 'It is the place where the Quicken Tree grows, the magic tree planted by the faerie people.'

'Would you like to go there?' asked Diarmaid.

Grainne took in her breath sharply.

'It is too dangerous,' she said, 'the tree is guarded by a great ogre and no one dares go near it.'

'Is that so?' said Diarmaid and laughed.

'Why are you laughing?' she asked.

'Because that is exactly why we must go there. For it is the one place where Finn will not pursue us.'

Grainne was worried by this plan for she feared the giant. But Diarmaid made light of her worries and said that if he approached the giant kindly, he might be able to strike a bargain with him. Failing that, he said, he was a match for any giant. In this way he persuaded Grainne to venture with him into the forest.

So they travelled on towards Dooros and, after a few days, looking down from a hillside, they saw its dark mass spread out below. The sun dropped behind the hill as they descended into the valley, and they arrived at the edge of the forest in the early evening gloom. Entering it, they began to move quietly between the thick-boled trunks of its trees. Above them the heavy branches were matted together, forming a dense canopy that blotted out the moonlight. They walked all night, afraid to lie down until the light came. But at the first touch of dawn, Grainne sank down on the bracken and Diarmaid let her sleep while he kept watch. Although he listened carefully, the wood seemed silent, almost too silent, for it seemed to him that no creatures rustled in its undergrowth and no birds sang.

When Grainne awoke, the couple set off once again for the heart of the forest. After a while they noticed that the trees were beginning to thin out and they could see where a bright light broke through and spilled into a glade ahead of them. Diarmaid put his hand on Grainne's arm.

'Be careful,' he warned, 'for we do not know about the powers of the tree, nor have we yet seen anything of the giant.'

Together they went warily towards the light-filled glade. As they approached it, Diarmaid became aware that the forest was beginning to become alive again. He could hear scuffling in the bracken, and a startled bird fluttered up with a thrill of beating wings.

When they reached the edge of the glade, they drew in their breath for they saw that the brightness was coming from a tree standing in the middle of it. The tree was throbbing with light and filling the whole glade with the sound of humming. It was holding out its branches like so many arms reaching towards them and each branch dripped with clusters of luminous ripe fruit, while a heavy scent of honey perfumed the air. Grainne started to go towards it, but Diarmaid held her back for already he had spotted something else. Beneath the tree was a hunched form like a great stone boulder. Round its waist was an iron chain and lying by its side, attached to the chain, was a great iron club. It was Sharvan the Surly, sitting motionless and watching them from a single, red, unblinking eye in the middle of his brow.

Grainne started back with a cry, but Diarmaid went boldly forward and bowed to the giant.

'Great Guardian of the Quicken Tree,' he said, 'we greet you with honour and respect. We have come to seek you out for we are in need of your help and protection.'

The giant curled his huge lip and waited.

'We have heard of your faithfulness in guarding the tree,' said Diarmaid, 'and so we know that you are one who can be trusted. Though it is true that many men fear you and dare not enter here because of you, nevertheless, we have come to throw ourselves on your mercy. We are fleeing the wrath of Finn, the great leader of the Fianna, and need refuge. If it seems good to you to kill us, then we can expect no better, but if you can let us live in peace, knowing that we will keep our distance and respect you, then we will do what we can to serve you.'

The giant blinked his eye and shifted his great bulk.

'The berries', he muttered, 'must not be taken.'

'That is so,' said Diarmaid, 'for they are in your charge. But if we promise you that we will never so much as touch a single berry, will you let us live in the forest with you, where we can be safe from pursuit?'

It took Diarmaid many hours of such persuasion, for the giant was a creature of few words and poor understanding, but such was Diarmaid's persistence that eventually the giant agreed to let the couple stay. They built a hut near a spring some distance from the magic glade and Diarmaid fenced it round with strong stakes interwoven with sapling branches, so that the couple began to feel at last that they were safe. Every day Diarmaid would go out hunting and each night he would bring back small animals for them to feed on. The nearer to the tree they went, however, the better were the pickings that they found and it was difficult indeed to avoid the glade itself and the searching eye of the giant. While Diarmaid was away, and Grainne was left alone in the hut, she sometimes felt as if she could hear the humming of the tree reaching out and calling to her.

The weeks went past and the couple lived happily together and enjoyed their love. Then a day came when Grainne told Diarmaid that she was expecting their child. After that Diarmaid began to take even greater care of Grainne, bringing her the richest food that he could find. But as the child grew inside her, the pull that she felt from the Quicken Tree grew stronger. Images of its berried branches began to haunt her. All day she longed for the taste of them and at night they came into her dreams. At last her craving was so strong that she told Diarmaid that she would die if she did not taste them, and she made him swear he would get some for her.

'And in case you should think badly of her,' said the harper, breaking off, 'let me remind you that we all crave the berries of the Quicken Tree, for they are filled with the power of life and with the wonder of youth.' Then she began to play a tune of such sweetness on her harp that the listeners felt as if the fruit itself was bursting on their tongues.

O, Quicken Tree, O Tree of Life
O, Quicken Tree, whose shining berries
hold out promise of Youth's loveliness.
O honey-scented one, red-fruited,
sprung from the faerie seed, juice-dripping.
Sweetness greets the tongue of all who taste you.

Bestower of life, love-giver,
radiant, berried one, you call,
while ancient forces guard your roots.
Only the hero, champion,
dares to fight and overcome
the fearful hindering guardian,
loosing your lovely juices and your fragrant fruits … ⑲

When she had bathed their spirits with the melting sounds of the music and the power of the life-giving fruit, the woman ceased her singing and laid her arms across her harp.

'Yet all this time,' she said, 'Finn was not idle. He guessed where the lovers were and was thinking of a plan to reach them.'

Putting her harp aside, she went on with the story.

Soon afterwards Finn summoned to him two chiefs of Leinster who owed him a debt of loyalty. He gave them this charge, to go into the Forest of Dooros and bring back either Diarmaid's dead body or a fistful of quicken berries. Unable to refuse, the men travelled to Dooros. They entered the forest cautiously knowing it was enchanted. Stealthily they made their way through it and were nearing the magic glade when they saw the lover's hut protected by its stout fence. They called to Diarmaid and asked him to come out and meet them in combat. Diarmaid laughed and, leaping suddenly over the fence, fell on one of them before he had time to unsheath his sword. He knocked him out with a blow and turned to the other man. After a short scuffle, he soon had them both bound and at his mercy. Then he told them they would have fared no better if they had tried to overcome the giant.

'For he is no ordinary foe,' he said. 'He can neither be burned with fire, nor drowned with water, nor can any weapon wound him except the blows from his own club.'

Hearing this the two chieftains tried to make peace by offering to help Diarmaid overcome the giant. But Diarmuid refused their help.

'Then will you take us to a place where we may watch you?' asked the men.

Diarmaid agreed to this and took the men to a hiding place near the glade. As they watched he went towards the giant, who was sleeping. He dealt him a blow at which the giant opened his red eye and glared at him in anger.

'I thought there was peace between us,' he growled. 'Are you now seeking to quarrel with me?'

'I have no wish to quarrel with you,' said Diarmaid, 'but I have come to ask you for a fistful of berries for my wife. She is with child and says she will die if she cannot taste them.'

'Even if she was carrying the last mortal child in the whole world,' replied the giant, 'I would not give her a single berry!'

As he spoke, he swayed to his feet and swung his club at Diarmaid. But Diarmaid dodged lightly out of the way. The giant swung again and struck him three times, but Diarmaid parried the blows with his shield as best he could. Then Diarmaid threw his weapons down and jumped on the giant, struggling with him until at last he threw him down with his bare hands. Snatching up the club, he dealt the giant three great blows with it, spilling out his brains. Afterwards Diarmaid swooned onto the ground, overcome by his own wounds. When he had recovered a little, he ordered the two chieftains to drag the giant's body away and bury it, and then to bring Grainne to him.

When Grainne came into the glade, he called out: 'See the quicken berries, Grainne. Now you can take some and eat them.'

But Grainne replied: 'I will not eat a single berry unless I receive it from your hand.'

So Diarmaid reached up and took a fistful of quicken berries and put them into her hand. Then he reached up again and gave the two chiefs a fistful to take back to Finn. After that, he ate some himself and his strength returned to him.

Diarmaid sent the two men back to Finn and told them to say that they had killed the giant themselves. The men returned to Finn's rath, but when they gave him the berries, he lifted them to his mouth and declared that he could smell the honeyed hand of Diarmaid on them. Guessing that the giant had been killed by Diarmaid and that the men had made peace with him, Finn rallied his men again and set out for Dooros. They journeyed swiftly and soon reached the forest. Coming to the glade of the Quicken Tree, and seeing that the giant was gone, they helped themselves to the berries and began to set up camp.

While his men busied themselves, Finn set up a table under the tree and spread a gaming board upon it. He sat down and began to play a game of *fidchell* with his son Oisin. Diarmaid and Grainne were hiding among the branches at the top of the tree and Diarmaid looked down on Finn as he sat below. He watched as he played one game and, towards the end of it, saw that Oisin was about to lose. As he reached the last move, Diarmaid dropped a berry on the board to show where his piece should go. Prompted by the falling berry Oisin made the move and won the game. Three times he played and three times he won by means of Diarmaid's falling berries. But it was not long before Finn realized what was happening. He dashed the board to the ground and called up angrily to Diarmaid, demanding that he show himself. In answer, Diarmaid parted the branches and gave Grainne three kisses. At this Finn fell into a great rage and in a loud voice offered riches and honour to any of his men who would climb up the tree and fetch Diarmaid down. The Fianna all hung their heads and refused. So Finn raised his voice and thundered out his offer again. This time a man called Garva, who had a grudge against Diarmaid's father, came forward and agreed to undertake the task.

As Garva began to ascend the tree, far away beside the Boyne, pain again swelled in the heart of Aengus Og. Sensing the lovers' plight, he flew to them a second time, landing invisibly in the top of the tree and offering, as before, to carry them both away. But again Diarmaid refused to be helped. So Aengus took Grainne to the safety of his palace while Diarmaid waited for Garva.

While Garva was still climbing the tree, Oscar began to plead with Finn for Diarmaid's life. As they argued, Diarmaid reached down and thrust Garva out of the tree so that he fell to his death below. More warriors from Garva's clan followed and Diarmaid threw them all down in the same way. Then Diarmaid took his two spears and leaped from the branch on which he stood. He soared high over the heads of the warriors and landed far beyond them. As soon as he touched the ground, he began to run, and this time Oscar decided to join him. Being the most fleet-footed of the Fianna, the two men soon left the other warriors far behind. After running for some miles they plunged down on the grass, heaving for breath, laughing and embracing each other.

The harper broke again from the story and began to play a light jig.

'Of course, Finn was very angry after this,' she said, 'and went on pursuing the couple for some time afterwards. But finally he listened to Oscar and the other members of the Fianna, who argued that, in the matter of love, it is always the younger man who must win in the end. And I am glad to say that after a long time, and with great reluctance, Finn stopped pursuing the lovers and returned home.'

When she had played her jig and another one or two besides, the people rose and ate again from the food they had brought with them while further flagons of wine were passed round. When they had eaten and drunk enough, and had walked about in order to lift the numbness from their limbs, they sat down again, and waited in silent expectation.

'And now,' said the woman, 'I have brought the lovers to the magic glade and I have told you of the new life quickening in Grainne's womb. They are at present in a place of peace and harmony, for Finn has ceased pursuing them. And I dare say there are some who would leave the story here. Nevertheless, the wheel of fate is ever turning in this world, and there is more to tell you. For, after rejoicing in the lovers' happiness, we must also share their sorrows. And so we come to the last part of our story. But, before it reaches its end, I have asked the Third Harper for his help again, for he knows well the powers that dance upon the threshold of the Otherworld.'

Then the woman bowed and, settling her harp upon her knee, began to play at the base of the strings, making a tight, rhythmic sound, like the noise of stones dropping in a shallow pool. When she spoke again, her voice seemed darker and more sonorous:

For sixteen years the couple lived happily and in peace and raised many children, but there came a day when Grainne said to Diarmaid: 'There is one thing that troubles me. One thing that spoils my happiness. For although we are now forgiven and accepted, we have never been invited to Finn's court or my father's court at Tara, nor have they visited us here. Surely the time has come for feasting and fellowship again. Let us send to both these great men and ask them to join us here with their retinues for a year of feasting.'

Diarmaid was uneasy at the thought of entertaining Finn under his roof. Nevertheless seeing that Grainne had set her heart on it, he agreed reluctantly, thinking that perhaps, after all, there could be no harm in it. So Grainne sent messengers to both courts and began making preparations for long months of hospitality. She was overjoyed when both Finn and Cormac sent back word saying they would come.

Soon afterwards the two companies arrived and spent their time hunting, carousing and feasting. There was much games-playing and merriment and Grainne rejoiced, for it seemed as if all that had rankled between them in the past was forgotten. But as the year was drawing to an end, Diarmaid was woken early one morning by the unexpected yelping of the hounds. Three times he heard their yelping and at last he rose from the bed telling Grainne he intended to join the hunt. But Grainne was troubled. She begged him to take his great spear and sword, the Red Javelin and the Great Fury. But Diarmaid was scornful of her request and went out with only the *Ga-boi* and the *Begallta*, the Yellow Javelin, and the Little Fury. As he went he gave a whistle and his hound Mac an Chuill bounded after him.

Diarmaid climbed to the top of the mountain of Ben Bulben, where he found the craggy figure of Finn waiting for him. Finn told him that his men had set out some hours before to hunt the famous boar of Ben Bulben but had lost its trail. He urged Diarmaid to go back, saying that thirty of his men had already been killed by the boar.

'I will not run from a wild pig,' said Diarmaid scornfully.

'That may be,' said Finn, 'but this is the earless and tail-less one that you are under *geis* never to hunt. It was your foster-father, Angus Og, who put that prohibition on you, knowing of the danger and your childhood prophecy.'

'What danger!' said Diarmaid scornfully. I know nothing of such childhood prophecies and will stay here with my hound and yours too, if you will lend him to me.'

But even as he spoke, they heard the fearful grunting of the great beast as it breasted the mountainside. At the sound of it, Finn and his hound, Bran, began descending the slope and were already halfway down and heading towards the valley, when the boar appeared.

The animal faltered as it came charging up the mountain.

For into its nostrils had come a scent and with it a half-formed memory, a name, a heart-beat. Words of power clanged in its ears and black wrath rose up in it. A roar came from its belly followed by a snarl of hatred. The creature scanned the grey horizon and saw a familiar shadowy figure standing on the bare flint of the mountainside alone.

Diarmaid waited until the huge beast was nearly on him before setting his hound at it, but at sight of the creature's huge tusks and wild eyes, the dog turned tail and ran. Then Diarmaid hurled the *Ga-boi* at the boar, but the spear bounced off its hide without leaving a mark. He drew the *Bagallta* and brought it down with all his weight on the boar's head. But the sword broke in two and the beast swerved and again charged towards him. Reaching for his shattered sword, Diarmaid wished with all his heart that he had with him his two great magic weapons. But now the boar was almost on him. As it leaped towards him Diarmaid seized hold of it with his bare hands, and plunged the jagged edge of the *Begallta* into its eye, driving it deep into his brain. At once the boar crashed down on top of Diarmaid, its great weight threatening to squeeze the life out of him. Diarmuid heaved at it until it rolled sideways onto the ground, where it lay thrashing in agony.

Finn came up then and saw Diarmaid lying on the mountainside, winded but still unblemished and beautiful, with the boar stretched out by his side, the blood welling from its wound. Then Finn became filled with his old jealous rage.

'Diarmaid,' he said, 'are you able to get up?'

Diarmaid rolled over on the screed away from the boar and raised himself up stiffly.

'Now,' said Finn, 'do you measure the boar.'

Diarmaid slowly paced the length of the boar.

'It is sixteen feet from tusk to heel,' he said.

'Measure it again against the hair,' said Finn, knowing of the mole on Diarmaid's foot.

So Diarmaid paced the boar again but, being unsteady from his fight, and feeling that his strength had left him, he stumbled as he laid his foot beside the boar. He tried to right himself and felt a sharp sting as one of the boar's bristles jabbed into his mole. As the poisoned hair entered him, he twisted on his ankle and fell back weakly on the ground.

As soon as he saw Diarmaid lying there Finn began to repent of his deed. He went up to him and asked what he could do.

Diarmaid replied, 'If I could drink water from the palms of Finn I would recover.'

So Finn went down the mountainside to where a spring gushed out of the rocks. He cupped some water in his hands, but as he came back to Diarmaid the thought of Grainne came strongly upon him so that he let it trickle out through his fingers. A second time Diarmaid begged him and a second time Finn went down to the spring, but again he let the water trickle away at the thought of Grainne. Then Diarmaid, who knew his life was fast leaving him, begged Finn a third time for the life-giving water. This time Finn ran to the spring in great haste and brought the healing water back to Diarmaid and let it drip into his mouth, but it was too late, for the water ran out of it and there was his pale body lying dead beside the boar.

As Finn stood looking down on his old enemy, the men of the Fianna came running up. When they saw that Diarmaid was dead,

Oscar, Oisin and Cailte took off their mantles and laid them over his body. Then Oscar spoke out against his grandfather:

'It would have been better if Diarmaid had lived and Finn himself had perished,' he said, 'for now the noblest heart in the Fianna has gone and we have lost our dearest comrade.' And all the men wept. Then, leaving the rest of the Fianna to guard the body, Oscar, Oisin and Cailte went back with Finn to the castle where Grainne was waiting.

As they approached the castle, they saw Grainne looking out from the ramparts. Seeing Finn leading her husband's hound, she said, 'Diarmaid cannot be coming if his hound is with Finn.' She leaned out and called to them anxiously for news of Diarmaid. When they told her he was dead she fainted and fell from the ramparts. She landed on the sward below the castle and all feared that she was dead. They carried her inside and when she came to herself again, she let out a great cry of sorrow for the death of Diarmaid, at which her women and all the household came running.

While some stayed behind to tend her, the main company went to Ben Bulben, climbing up the mountain until they found Diarmaid's body. As they looked down on their dead lord, they heard loud wing-beats as if from a huge flock of swans, and saw Aengus Og coming towards them carried on the cold wind, and a great crowd of the Tuatha with him. He alighted on the mountainside and went to Diarmaid. Then, weeping over his fair and lifeless body, he spoke these words:

'Alas, Diarmaid, you were to me as my own soul. Ever since you were put into my care at the *Brugh*, I have watched over you. Not one night has gone by without my guarding you, except for the one night that is gone. O Diarmaid, bitter it is to me that for the one night I failed to guard you, death laid its dreadful hand upon you.'

Then Aengus and all the company of people gave three great bitter cries of sorrow which ascended as high as the heavens and reverberated throughout the waste places below the earth.

Afterwards Aengus ordered that Diarmaid's body be taken to the *Brugh na Boyne,* and Grainne's people gave their consent. So Diarmaid was lifted gently and wrapped in costly garments. Then he was laid on a golden bier flanked by his spears and javelins pointing towards the sky. In this way he was borne to Aengus' palace, where his body was laid with ceremony in the Great Hall. Then Aengus knelt and gazed on the fair face of his foster-son and, with tears running from his eyes, began to speak this lament.

The Third Harper came forward carrying a set of pipes. He struck up a drone while the woman played and spoke these words:

Alas, Diarmaid of the bright face,
chief in courage among the Fianna
fair warrior of the white teeth,
and the darling of women.
O Diarmaid of the fair brow,
Diarmaid, my heart's soul
slain by the treachery of Finn!

Alas, Diarmaid,
for the life has left you
numbing poison has held you in its arms.

The wild boar in his fierceness
has laid you low, O Diarmaid of the bright weapons. ⑳

The harper bowed his head and ceased his playing. But the plaintive sounds continued, carried by the woman's silvery harp, shivering and crying round the cave. And, caught up in the wail strain, all who listened wept, mourning the deaths of their own kin, and their own lost youth.

While they wept, they heard the woman's voice ringing out above their wailing: 'But though Aengus was unable to bring Diarmaid back to life, such was the power of the god that he was able to breath a spirit into him. And so Aengus raised up Diarmaid and was able to talk with him for a little while each day.'

As her voice died away, the people continued weeping, for the weight of sorrow was still upon them. But now they wept for the golden age that was past, for the glories of the Fianna, the power of the gods, the love of the goddess, and the wisdom of the kings of old.

When, at last, they had wept their fill, they saw that the three bards had gone, and the quiet rhythm of the waves had claimed the cave once more. Slowly they came back to life and began to gather up their cloaks and their belongings. As they made their way out of the cave, they looked up and saw that high above them hung a crescent moon with a single, lingering star caught within her crook. And as they walked stiff-limbed towards their boats, all around them rose a pale and fragile light, the fledgling herald of a newborn day.

CYMRU

Cymru is the Celtic name for Wales. The Welsh manuscripts are later in date than the Irish, the main ones being the *White Book of Rhydderch* (c.1325) and the *Red Book of Hergest* (c.1400). There are fewer Welsh myths than Irish, and most of them are contained in the Mabinogion, which was compiled by Lady Charlotte Guest in the nineteenth century. The *Mabinogi* proper contains four main branches, or stories, concerning Pwyll, Branwen, Manawydan and Math. Many editions, however, include seven further tales, of which three are early Arthurian ones. The tales in this section come from the first and fourth branches of the *Mabinogi*. The Story of Taliesin is found in a thirteenth-century manuscript, the *Hanes Taliesin*.

PROLOGUE

I do not know how old the druid is, or how many incarnations he has had. He speaks of many, but whether they were in body or in spirit I cannot tell. His beard is white, his skin wrinkled and his hair like a mass of silver cobwebs round his face. But his eyes are young.

I have been travelling with him for two quarters of the year – ever since the feast of Beltain, when the people bless the land with their dancing and the branches of hawthorn are brought into the houses. I am part companion to him, and part apprentice, for he has undertaken to teach me the Druid Mysteries.

When Gwydion asked for a companion and I was chosen, I could hardly believe it. For he is the greatest druid and magician that we have still living. I had heard tales that in his youth he was a cunning trickster and used his magic to outwit great kings and even the Goddess herself. So, at first, although I felt greatly honoured I was wary of him, until one day he said to me: 'Do not believe everything you hear, Gwyn. Keep your mind open and listen for the truth yourself.'

Since then I have learned much and feel a great kinship with him.

Now he has promised to tell me how he mastered the three tests of bard, seer and druid. There were no druid colleges in those days, so he learned from a master, his uncle Math. I must listen well, because I may be the last alive to hear his story from his own lips. I must hold it in my memory so that those who come in later times can learn his wisdom, for already his name is passing into legend …

22
Pwyll and the Lord of Annwn

It was dusk when I entered the sacred oak grove. Gwydion had built a fire in the middle of it and the strange curve of his harp was silhouetted against its flames. As I came up, he was striking chords on it and chanting:

Arawn, great lord, wild hunter,
leader of the ghostly hounds,
white-pelted, luminescent,
with ears like dancing flame.
Great Cerne, horned god, club wielding
Fierce master of the wildwood,
Wise guardian of all creatures,
Dark Ruler of Annwn. (21)

He broke off when he saw me and patted the ground with his staff. After I had sat down beside him, he smiled.

'There are many ways of knowing when you are on the threshold of Annwn,' he said.

'You may hear the singing of the Birds of Rhiannon – and after that you will never relish any other music. You may find yourself suddenly surrounded by a strange and unexpected mist. Or you may encounter white animals – creatures of the threshold.'

He paused.

'When you see all or any of these signs beware, for you are at the portals of the Otherworld!'

Then, fixing his grey eyes upon me, he began his story:

When Pwyll, the young lord of Dyfed, came to the gateway of Annwn he ignored such signs. He was hunting in the woods of Glen Cuch with his companions, following a stag. They lost it and he became separated from his companions. Then suddenly there it was again, a large white beast crashing through the branches, keeping out of sight. Soon his hounds were in hot pursuit. They tracked the beast deeper and deeper into the heart of the forest. Then all at once an unearthly howling filled the air. The hounds stopped, their ears taut and their nostrils quivering. Pwyll tore after them into the clearing, and saw at last the white stag he had chased. But close upon it were a pack of bloodless hounds, their white hair bristling and their crimson ears glowing. They leaped on the animal and brought it down. But Pwyll charged towards them and drove them off. Then, blasting on his horn he called up his own hounds and, soon afterwards, yelping loudly, they rushed into the glade and baited upon the beast.

No sooner had they done so than a long, low note rang out and echoed round the forest. The white hounds gathered together at the sound, their fiery ears erect. A huge horse, dapple-grey and heavy-hoofed burst through the undergrowth and into the clearing. On its back was a swarthy lord, with black hair flowing down his back, an earth-coloured cloak flying from his shoulders and a long bronze hunting horn hanging at his breast. Pwyll looked at the man and, for a brief moment, thought he saw the antlered branches of a tree spring from his head. Then the illusion vanished.

The dark horseman galloped up to Pwyll and reined in his horse sharply.

'Stranger, I will not greet you!' he cried.

'Why not?' asked Pwyll, 'Does your rank prevent it?'

'No,' said the stranger, 'It is because you have dishonoured me by driving off my hounds.'

He glared at Pwyll. ' The price of such an insult is a hundred stags!'

Pwyll was about to give a hot reply but checked himself and looked again at the alien pack. This time he saw their whiteness and the unearthly light that came from them.

He faced the stranger.

'You are right,' he said, 'I have, indeed, been high-handed and I would like to make amends.'

He dismounted. The horseman also dismounted and they came towards each other.

'There is a service you could do for me,' said the stranger.

'Tell me what it is and I will gladly do it.'

'Hafgan, my rival, rules the land that borders mine. He is a trouble to my kingdom and although each year we meet in combat, I am unable to kill him for our strengths are equal. But you would find it easy to kill him.

'How shall I do it?' asked Pwyll.

'First we will take an oath of friendship and then change places for a year and a day. We must exchange our likenesses so that no one will know of our arrangement. You shall rule my kingdom of Annwn, and I shall rule your kingdom of Dyfed.

If you agree to this, 'he added,' the most beautiful woman in the world will be your companion day and night.'

'If you will tell me how to rid you of Hafgan, I will accept your terms,' said Pwyll.

'Good,' said the other. 'The time of the next conflict is a year and a day from now. Deal him one blow and you will kill him. But only strike him once, however much he begs you.'

Pwyll agreed and the men exchanged oaths.

'And now,' said the dark lord, 'you and I must also exchange our likenesses.'

As he spoke a mist rose up around them. Pwyll felt its moist breath stealing over him, and became aware of a prickling of his skin, a tightening of his brow, a lengthening of his limbs. The mist cleared suddenly and he stared in astonishment, for the face that looked at him was his own. Drawing in his breath, he looked down at his arms and saw they were black-haired and swarthy.

Then his face smiled at him and his voice said: 'You see we now have each other's semblance. You are Lord of Annwn, and I am Pwyll, Lord of Dyfed. No one will know of our exchange, for we will rule each other's kingdoms perfectly.'

'And now,' said his own voice again, 'Mount my horse and I will show you the gateway to my kingdom.'

Arawn led him to an archway formed by two trees whose tightly woven branches kept the sun at bay. There the two men clasped hands. Then Arawn touched his whip to the horse which straightaway galloped through the archway and down into blackness.

Pwyll rode through the darkness, and came out into a fair land lit by a silver sun. Ahead of him was a huge white castle, fresh and shining as if the dew still lay upon it. Birdsong, sweet and mellow, filled the air, and the land stretched away to the horizon in a streak of purple. All around were fine white mansions, towers, courtyards and stately houses.

As he rode towards the palace gates, two servants came out to greet him. One took his horse and the other pulled of his boots then led him inside the palace where he was shown to a chamber decorated with costly hangings. He bathed himself in a marble basin and put on a silk tunic stiff with gold embroidery.

Dressed in Arawn's robes and displaying Arawn's stern bearing and commanding gaze, he entered the Great Hall. It was even more splendid than his own. Flags hung down its length, and shields of beaten copper caught the firelight. The panelled walls were lined with long oak tables laden with stuffed meats, fine fruits and delicacies and jars of wine. As Pwyll walked down the hall between the tables, a woman dressed in a long robe of yellow silk came towards him, and held out her hand.

He looked at her in wonder, for she was more beautiful than he had imagined. Her hair was bright as burnished bronze, her face pale and her eyes blue as a mountain lake. He took her hand and tried to stop his own from trembling as she led him to his regal seat. While they feasted he gazed around at the richness of the court. But most of all he marvelled at the woman who sat beside him, and whose wit and conversation were as dazzling as her beauty.

That night, when the feasting was done, she led him to their chamber and turned to him with shining eyes. Desire came upon him and he reached for her. But as he did so the image of the dying stag rose up before him. He remembered how his hounds had baited upon it, and he thought of the high price he paid for plundering the riches of Annwn. All this passed swiftly through his mind, and he held back from her.

So it was that, though he saw the hurt in her eyes, and though he longed for her with a great passion, Pwyll reined in his desire and kept from touching her the whole year he was king.

But in that year he ruled the land as well as if its dark lord had never left it. He grew to love the land and its people and so the time passed happily enough. And when the day of combat came, he went out with a retinue of men to meet King Hafgan.

Flanked by their armies, the two kings faced each other across the ford. As soon as they heard the signal, they charged at each other and Pwyll struck Hafgan a single mighty blow that split his shield in two and ripped through his armour. Such was its force that it threw King Hafgan over the rump of his horse and into the river, where he lay half-dead, his wounds bleeding freely in the water.

'Have pity on me,' cried the king. 'Strike me again that I may die more quickly!'

When Pwyll refused, Hafgan looked at him and realization flickered in his eyes.

'What right had you to slay me?' he asked. 'I had no quarrel with you.'

Then he sank back and closed his eyes and his men came and carried him away.

Pwyll strode forward and addressed the assembled soldiers.

'Your king is dead,' he said, 'I have killed him in fair combat. Now you must decide if you will submit to me in peace. If not, I shall have to take you by force!'

Hafgan's soldiers immediately bowed to him and paid him homage. Afterwards, his dark eyes blazing in triumph, Pwyll led both armies round the dead king's land, and subdued every town and village to his rule.

Next day at noon he arrived at the meeting place in the woods of Glyn Cuch and found Arawn waiting for him. The two men embraced each other. Now they were more than friends or brothers, for each man had the measure of each other's worlds – and they were one. After they embraced, Arawn restored Pwyll to his own likeness and took back his own dark bearing. Then the two men rode back to their own kingdoms.

On his return, Arawn was overjoyed to see his wife and his old companions again. Nevertheless, he behaved as if he had only gone a day from his kingdom. But that night when he went into his chamber and took his wife in his arms, instead of responding to him, she remained rigid while the colour came and went in her cheeks. When, after caressing her and speaking words of love to her, she still failed to respond, he lay down in wonder. He slept for a while, then woke again and saw her lying beside him deep in thought. He put out a hand to touch her and spoke to her again, but she remained silent. A third time he woke and spoke to her, but she said not a word.

'Why won't you speak to me?' he asked.

'For a whole year,' she replied, 'not one word has passed between us in this place.'

'But we always talk together,' he said.

'I swear,' she answered, 'that from the moment we lay down on our beds until we rose again next morning, not one word passed between us, let alone anything else.'

Arawn remained marvelling for a while. Then he said:

'Lady, don't be angry with me, for I swear I have neither lain down with you nor slept with you for a whole year.' And he told her of his bargain with Pwyll.

'By heaven,' she said, 'you must have a strong bond with such a man, if he could keep such faith with you.'

'That was what I was thinking,' said Arawn,

Meanwhile Pwyll had also returned to his own kingdom where he found everything in good order. He asked his men if they felt he had ruled well during the past year. They replied that he had shown outstanding kindness and wisdom, and had been even more generous in distributing his goods.

'Then it is not me you should thank, but the man who took my place,' said Pwyll and told them of the pact between himself and Arawn.

The men were astonished at the tale, and when he had finished, asked him anxiously whether he would uphold the new ruling. Pwyll promised he would rule his kingdom as generously as Arawn himself. And, once the story of his uniting the two kingdoms became known, it not long before his people began to call him Pwyll, lord of Annwn.'

Gwydion looked up.

'And from that time onwards the two men continued their friendship and sent each other gifts and riches, the bounties of their kingdoms.'

He stroked the symbols on his staff.

'A free exchange between the worlds,' he muttered.

Then he reached again for his harp and began to chant:

Yn Annwn y diwyth
yn Annwn y gorwyth
yn Annwn is eluyd.

Annwn the land of peace
Annwn the land of trial
Annwn, the kingdom underneath the earth.

23

Gwydion's Story

When I woke next morning, I found that Gwydion had already left the hut. As I hurried to the oak grove I could hear him singing. There was power and excitement in his voice. This is what he sang:

A new strength came to me.
Its power was in my voice, my step, my covering.
The wildness of the hunt, the skills of bird and beast –
the horn, the hoof, the fierce unbounded freedom
and the savage understanding. All were mine.
My heart beat strongly. In my new-found might
I raised my antlered head and bellowed at the moon (22)

When he had finished he smiled at me. His eyes were shining.

'And now we come to my own story,' he said.

My heart beat fast when I heard this, for it was the very thing I had been waiting for – Gwydion's story told from his own lips. I had heard the tale already but found it difficult to understand. Besides that, it had shown the druid in a bad light.

As if he read my thoughts, Gwydion said:

'I expect you have already heard it – at least in part.'

I nodded.

'So you will know that I had my training at the court of my uncle, King Math. And you may also know that, because of Math's magical constraint, my brother Gilvaethwy and I used to travel round his cantrevs and inspect his kingdom for him.'

I nodded again.

'And you will have heard, perhaps, of his constraint,' he said. 'That unless he had his feet resting in the lap of a young virgin, he would die. Or at least that is what he told us. The only time he might break this *geis* was if he went to war.'

Gwydion paused.

'I expect you know what use I made of that!'

When he saw the guarded look on my face, he gave a short laugh.

'There is another way to look at it,' he said.

As I sat trembling with anticipation, he settled himself back against the oak tree and closed his eyes.

A brother, yet closer than a brother was Gilvaethwy. I remember we were in the Great Hall, with the rush light guttering. In his huge seat, King Math, his heavy cloak folded on his shoulders, had his feet stretched out, large and bare. And she, Goewin, the pure untouched one, was cradling them between her knees.

'It is not right,' said my brother to me with his eyes.

Soul of my soul he was to me. I felt his anger stirring as he watched the woman, pale-faced, yellow-haired, bending to kiss the king's old feet. But I saw that behind his anger there was something else. I motioned to him and we left the hall.

Outside the palace I looked at Gilvaethwy and raised a brow enquiringly. His eyes darted one way then the other while he put a finger to his lips. We both knew what he meant. The old king possessed a sorcery so that what was told in secret was carried to him on the wind – the slightest breeze would take even a whisper to his ear. And so, ancient though he was, Math still held the land in his thrall, for no word of treachery could pass without his hearing it.

I looked at my brother and saw how thin and pale he had become – like the virgin girl herself.

'It is about her!' I said.

In answer I saw him tremble and then I understood. Behind the passion of anger was the passion of desire. I came close to him and looked deep into his eyes.

'Leave it to me,' I said.

Next day I went to Math. I saw her at his feet, giving him her power, the power of the land. And yet he was too old to be her consort. I looked at her and I agreed with Gilvaethwy. It was not right.

'Gwydion,' said Math, 'you asked to see me. Is there something on your mind?'

I gathered my thoughts.

'I have heard, Lord, that there are some wonderful new creatures that have arrived in the kingdom of Dyfed.' I said.

'What are they called?' asked Math.

'Pigs, lord.'

'Tell me about them,' said the king.

'Their flesh is sweeter and more tender than the flesh of cows.'

'Whose are they?' asked Math.

'They were a present from Arawn, King of Annwn, to Pryderi, son of Pwyll.'

'Then they are new to this world', said Math, looking thoughtful.

He was thinking about how Arawn had once had a special

friendship with Pryderi's father, Pwyll. Now the father was dead, Arawn gave gifts to the son. But I suspected the son did not always understand the value of such gifts.

'Let me go and ask for them,' I said. I was thinking again of the pigs.

'What makes you think he will give them to you?' asked Math.

'I will go in disguise,' I answered, 'I will go as a bard in a band of bards.'

'Even so,' said Math, 'how do you know you will succeed?'

'Because my plan is good,' I said.

So Math gave me eleven men and we travelled south to Pryderi's court, galloping across gorse-covered plains and picking our way among the foothills. Before us, on the horizon lay the reclining limbs of the great goddess. When, at last, we reached her lowest crags, we dismounted and led our horses over her steep passes. It was hard going, but after many hours, we finally came out on the bounding hills and wooded plains of Dyfed.

At Pryderi's court we were given a great welcome. The King was kind to us and I almost felt sorry for what I purposed. But then I saw the piglets. Black with pink udders, their small eyes blinking at the light. Pryderi laughed, amused by them.

'A gift,' he said, 'from Arawn. Remarkable, really, the old king still being faithful, after all these years.'

I smiled and looked again at the piglets. I saw their instinct, and their secret knowing. One day they would be prized, the hero's portion at the feast. But Pryderi saw nothing of this. I vowed to myself again that if he broke his promise to Arawn, I would take them.

That night we dined in his feasting hall. While we ate, jugglers, fools and minstrels entertained us. Then Pryderi turned to me and asked for a story. I rose from my seat and went to the middle of the hall. I sat and stroked my harp. I coaxed from it sweet melodies and tear-making tales, the finest in my repertoire. Then I spoke this riddle:

> The beast that keeps the threshold
> of the Underworld has come.
> Its eyes are small, it scents the earth
> and seeks out hidden gateways.
> Sacred places are its haunt.
> It hails from deepest darkness
> where the unborn power begins –
> the realm where lies the deepest
> and most ancient understanding.
> The realm where lies the Word [23]

As I sang I was summoning the pigs with my bardic power in front of the king's entire host. All the court heard me, yet no one understood the meaning of my song.

Afterwards I went back to my place beside Pryderi, who was fulsome in his praise.

'Yours is a rare and marvellous talent,' he said, 'and such talent should not go unrewarded.'

I looked him boldly in the eye.

'I have heard that some wonderful new creatures have come into your possession, gifts from Arawn,' I said. 'I have come to ask you for them.'

'I am not able to give them to you,' he replied 'for I have pledged to keep them until they have doubled in number.'

I smiled and said to him: 'There is a way that I can release you from that pledge. Wait until the morning and I will show you.'

In the middle of the night I left my chamber and stole out quietly. I went to a lonely place at the edge of the palace grounds. I marked the earth with my staff and summoned my bardic magic. By daybreak I had conjured twelve stallions with gold saddles and bridles and twelve white-breasted greyhounds with gold collars and leads. I had also transformed twelve toadstools that were growing in a hollow tree into twelve golden shields.

Next morning I brought these wonders into the court and presented them to Pryderi.

'Lord,' I said, 'I have made good my promise. Now I put it to you, although you have pledged not to give away your pigs, may you not instead exchange them for something better?'

In answer, the king summoned his counsellors to a meeting and, after much debate, they decided to accept my offer. As soon as I knew the pigs were mine, I made my excuses and hurriedly left the court with my band of bards.

We travelled back as quickly as we could, knowing that the illusion would only last a day. But driving the pigs through the mountain passes was difficult and it was several days before we arrived back at the court of Caer Dathyl.

There we found Math preparing for battle. He told us that Pryderi had raised an army against us because of the theft of the pigs.

Quickly equipping ourselves for war, my brother and I took our places in Math's army. We marched with them for a day, but as soon as it was dark, we crept out of the camp and stole back to the court under the cover of night.

We left our horses in the stable-yard and went inside. 'It was time', we told ourselves, 'to release the Virgin into the Mother'. There were only women left at the palace and we herded them screaming into one room. Then, while I kept the door against the women, Gilvaethwy went into Goewin and forced himself on her. Afterwards we rode back, still swathed by night, and returned unnoticed to our places in Math's army.

Gwydion sighed. He looked at me and the message in his eyes told me to hold my judgement. Then he returned to the inner vision of his mind.

The battle raged between our men and Pryderi's. For two days they put up a good fight and on the third we routed them and they fled. We pursued them until they surrendered to us and then we took hostages. But the men on both sides were angry and skirmishes kept breaking out between our armies.

At last Pryderi sent messengers, challenging me to single combat. He said that it was a matter between the two of us – and it was true. For I was the challenger to his Otherworldly powers.

Watched intently by both armies, we circled each other warily. Pryderi was skilled in arms and I in bardic lore. I raised my sword, he drew his and our blades clashed. I felt his heaviness, his powerful wrists and the full weight of his shoulder lying behind each stroke. He had the strength, the training. But I had the nimbleness, the cunning. I dodged his blows and fought fair until my strength began to wane. Then I called up my magic and at once my sword began to dance in my hand. Mirroring its own light-points, a second sword sprang up. It was an illusion. Pryderi parried a flash of silver blade, but nothing bit his sword-edge. As my double-weapon flickered round his head, he began slashing wildly at the stabbing beams of light.

'What good is all your martial training to you now?' I thought.

I saw his mind become confused. He put up a brave fight, I will give him that. He was skilled and stout-hearted. But it was not enough. In his efforts to parry my illusions, he missed the true edge of my sword. I struck him once and it was a clean stroke. He staggered and fell. The fight was over.

Immediately a cheer went up from our men and a wail of grief from the others. I caught Math looking at me and for a moment I wondered if he had known all along how it would be.

Leaving the enemy to bury their king, we turned for home triumphant. Math was lord of a new land, and I of an Otherworldly kingdom.

As soon as we were back at Caer Dathyl, Math called for Goewin to hold his feet. She came to him tearful but with the light of woman on her.

'You must find another virgin to hold your feet, Lord,' she said, 'for that is my state no longer. But I swear to you, Lord, that I did not betray you, for I was taken against my will.'

After Math heard her story he became very angry and looked about for my brother and myself. But we had already gone to inspect his cantrevs.

We travelled quickly west, but word went round and the villagers closed their doors against us. We were made to fast, for none would feed us. Driven by need we made our way back home.

Gwydion looked at me.

'At least that is what they say,' he said, 'that we were driven back reluctantly to accept our punishment.'

'And what was your punishment?' I asked.

'Math changed us into wild beasts.'

He saw the look on my face.

'You think that is a great disgrace,' he said, 'I tell you it was the highest honour.'

When I looked at him in surprise, he said, 'It was because I had won Pryderi's kingdom and had proved my readiness. We were not driven home by hunger, nor did we submit to punishment. We came back willingly. Our fast was a preparation.'

He reached for his harp and played a delicate melody, picking out individual notes with care and skill. Then he said:

Math raised his wand and touched me with it. It was the first magic – the oldest magic. My flanks enlarged. I was thrust forward on all fours. My back extended, antlers pushed from my brow, my ears stood up erect, my snout became soft and wide. I dipped my head and licked my hoof with my tongue. Then we were off. Galloping over the rush matting of the hall, making for the smells and sounds and earthy flooring of the forest.

He played the careful notes again, speaking while he played:

Dapple-coated, warm, smooth-flanked, a delicate lord among the trees, I quivered at a twig's crack, kept aware when sleeping, one ear taut and listening. As for my brother Gilvaethwy, 'Soul of my soul', I called him. Now he became 'Body of my body'. As Math had ordered, we became one flesh. I was the stag and he the hind. We rutted in the rich decay of leaves and knew the joy of offspring. One small calf we birthed. And while Gilvaethwy tended it, I learned its guardianship. Power of sun lay in us, for our branching antlers were its rays. Proudly we bore upon our heads its crown of wisdom. Flickering in the boughs and undergrowth like shadows, we learned the ways of forest, felt its paths, its ways, its tree-lore. Then all too soon, it seemed, we heard our summoning.

We went back to the palace, clattering our hooves on the cobblestones of the yard and setting the guard dogs barking. Math came out and touched our young one with his staff, turning it into a boy. Then he laid his staff on us and our second shape-changing began.

Gwydion played again. This time his chords were thick, his tune stouter and more ponderous.

At first we seemed to shrivel up, especially our snouts. Our vision shortened like our flanks. But our sense of smell grew stronger as we felt our nostrils nudge the earth. I became soft-bellied, dugs hung from me, and with them a strange, instinctual knowing. As I raised my head, Gilvaethwy lifted up his powerful face. I saw he had two great tusks. And now it was he who overpowered me, he who gave me young. I learned the power of birth, the mute pull of tender mouths sucking on my dugs, the surge of new milk flowing through my body. My belly was the earth, its womb my own. I had its understanding and I knew its secrets.

All too soon the summoning came again. Another year had passed. We went back to the palace, our trotters slipping on the cobbles and our piglet with us, waiting for the barking of the dogs to bring the king. When he came, he touched the piglet with his staff and made it human. Then he touched our shoulders. And our third shape-change began.

Again, Gwydion took up his harp. This time he struck music from its lowest strings raising a fierce melody, which growled and buzzed about my ear.

Lean and lifted higher from the ground, my eyes became keen, my hair rough. My snout grew longer. When I bared my teeth, a threatening sound of thunder came from me. I was lithe-limbed, powerful and cruel. When I snapped my jaws even Math flinched. My tail hung low and curved. I was all stealth, ferocity and wildness. With a snarl, I bounded from the hall and headed for the woods and mountain slopes.

Now it was not so much the moist darkness of the earth that called me, as the black sky and the silver torc of the moon. I cried against it, waiting for its pale disk to show my likeness in its shadowing. I felt the strength and power of the male, but the hidden passions of the night were mine as well. Thus came my magic. We formed a pack, my brother and I. We raised our cubs and howled and ran together.

Then the summons came again. Another year had passed. We leaped onto the cobbles of the palace, out-faced the guard dogs with our fearful fangs, our white-rimmed eyes. Math came and found us, touched our cub and made it human. Then he turned to us. As he raised his staff our litheness left us, panting tongues, sleek flanks, pad-footedness - all fell away. The fertile earth, its scents and secrets, gave up its pull. We stumbled on two legs. We eyed each other. We were men again.

When we had washed ourselves and dined with Math and he had seen the white gleam of our eyes, the cunning on our faces and our new-found wariness, he called us to his chamber.

'Men!' he said, 'Now that you have new wisdom, I need your advice.'

He looked at each of us.

'I need a new virgin foot-holder to guard my feet. Who shall I ask to take this post?'

Even before he had finished speaking, a vision rose in me, and a name burst from my lips:

'Arianrhod!' I said.

24
Arianrhod's Story

Next morning I rose early for I could hardly wait to hear more of Gwydion's story. But when we sat down in the sacred grove, I saw his face was troubled.

'What do you know of the Goddess?' he asked, his grizzled mane of hair shadowing his face.

'She is the earth,' I replied.

'And what else do you know of her?' he asked.

'She is Sovereignty and to wed her is to wed the land itself.'

'Ah! That is the meaning of kingship,' said Gwydion.

There was silence between us. Then he spoke again.

'And so she chooses her consort, does she not?'

'Of course!' I replied.

'Not since she has been dishonoured,' he said sharply.

I looked at him and saw the anxiety in his eyes.

'Gwyn,' he said, 'it is not enough to say that the Goddess is the earth. You must also know how she manifests herself.'

The blood came to my cheeks and I looked away. I was ashamed because I did not know. Gwydion sighed.

'These are sad days,' he said, 'now that men have chosen to forget her.'

He took my hand and gripped it.

'But it is your task to understand her teachings and to keep her wisdom in your heart.'

With these words he unwrapped his harp and began to play a sweet and fragile melody. Then he spoke in a voice half-speech, half-singing, over the music.

On an island off our western shore, there is a magically turning glass castle. Inside it lives a goddess of the moon and stars. The castle turns and the goddess turns with it. She also turns with the seasons. With the spring she is a young untouched maiden. With the summer she is a full-bosomed mother, fruitful and nurturing, and with the cold winter season she becomes withered and grey, but wise as the feathered owl – an old crone, indeed. Then, next spring, she returns, a beautiful virgin maiden, renewed and resplendent. And this is the way of all goddesses, for they mirror the land and its seasonal round.

He put his harp aside.

'Many moons ago, men understood this and worshipped the Goddess in her three aspects, knowing that as long as she kept changing and renewing herself, then so, too, would the seasons.'

He looked at me and his eyes were burning.

'I knew this,' he said, 'and she knew this, but the men about us had forgotten. They told themselves that it was they who ordered the earth, they who commanded its fruitfulness by their sowing and tilling, and they who owned their women and chose the birthing of their children.' He paused. 'But she knew that they were wrong!'

'Who was she?' I asked.

'You mean the goddess on the island?' he said.

I nodded.

'My sister Arianrhod,' he replied.

He smiled and his eyes softened.

'Which is why I suggested her for the post of Math's virgin foot-holder.'

He settled himself again and spread his robe round him on the bracken. 'And now I will tell you her part of the story,' he said.

Gwydion raised his eyes to the sky. Then he reached for his harp and, drawing a delicate rhythm from it, spoke his sister's words:

I, Arianrhod, chaste Goddess of the Moon
dwell in *Caer Sidi*,
the Castle of Glass, alone.
Three fountains rise before my chair,
three rings of fire surround my bower.
Who dares ascend the Seat of Awen
in my tower?

Bards journey here for the flickering fire –
most precious, most rare,
that touches the spirit, that poets inspire.
And I, Arianrhod, am guardian of the tower
whose glass is my womb
and whose seat is my bower.

Long and white are my fingers,
I unplait my hair
in the light of the moon
and ascend to my chair.
Is it not my chaste beauty
the flame of desire,

that draws the great seers
to my close-guarded fire. ㉔

As he sang, a rocky island rose up before me, its high tower spearing the sky. I saw within it a beautiful woman, fair as the stars but cold and distant as the moon.

Gwydion put the harp down. He said:

At Math's bidding, I took a boat and sailed down the coast to Arianrhod's island. As I beached it on her shore, I looked up. High above me flashed the turning castle, its glass windows reflecting the rays of the midday sun. The tower was turning as slowly as the seasons. At its heart pulsed the *awen*, the Seat of Inspiration. Three fires burned perpetually before it – this much I knew. I could see their smoke rising from the blackened eyelets at the crest of the tower. I began to climb the narrow path, which wound snakelike between boulders of harsh black rock. When I reached the courtyard, three great fountains stood before me, throwing veils of silver water in the air. As I passed between them I felt their spray fall on me like a watery baptism.

I entered the great gateway and Arianrhod herself came out to meet me. A long blue robe was wound around her slender body, while a white cloak fell in folds from her shoulders. Her long dark hair was caught inside a silver crown speared with a single crescent moon.

Gwydion's eyes filled with tears.

Then she, who was more than sister to me, she who was goddess of the silver wheel, the starry web itself – took me in her arms. And I felt the world turn within me, I felt the power of sun mount in my heart, the flame of a god's desire.

She led me through the hall and we approached the burning place, the beating, pulsing centre, the flaring seat of inspiration with its guardian flames. Still wet from my baptism of water, I passed through the fire and, at a sign from her, ascended the crystal seat. The touch of the flames was on me and their smoke swathed my eyes. In their swirling shapes I saw rising images, the wand of Math and the Child of the Wave. Then they rode away on the smoke. After that I saw the crown-bearing one, the Sacred Child. But as I bent to see his face, an eagle passed before it lifting a shadowing wing. The smoke whirled more thickly round my eyes and then I saw, reaching to the sky, a thickly branched tree with birds clustered upon it. But before I could hear their song, the tree was snatched away and in its place I saw a great chasm. It was the heart of the fire, the black pit from which arose its smoke – a place of awe, a crevice between rocks, a cave of Unknowing. I drew back in fear, stumbling from the throne. Then I pitched forward, sightless, and fell through the fire into Arianrhod's arms.

She smiled at me, singed and blackened as I was.

'That was well-endured,' she said.

That night she took me to walk on the beach. The moonlight stretched across the water like a sheet of silk. We lay on the pale sand beneath the wheel of stars, and she took me in her arms again.

The druid closed his eyes.

'Remember what I told you about the Goddess – that she is

always Virgin, for she renews herself each spring,' he said.

He handed me the leather flask he carried on his belt. We both drank from it. Then, with a sigh, he continued his story.

It was late spring, bordering on summer, when we travelled back to Math's court at Caer Dathal. Arianrhod held her head high and a fierce light burned in her eyes. She was a proud woman, proud of her goddess heritage and her powers. We journeyed towards the court with high hopes, and not even I could foresee at that time what would happen to her.

When we arrived at the court, Arianrhod was treated with every honour before being ushered into Math's presence. I remember how she stepped down the length of the Great Hall, all eyes upon her. She wore a white robe that trailed over the rush-strewn floor, her dark blue cloak was draped across her shoulders and her hair, coiled like dark snakes, was caught within her silver crown.

She went up to the huge figure of Math as he sat on his throne of polished marble, and bowed her head stiffly. It was an acknowledgement from the goddess to the god. In answer he looked her up and down. When he spoke, his voice was edged.

'Lady,' he said, 'I have need of a virgin. I believe you are such a one.'

Arianrhod looked at him coolly.

'My lord, I have known no other than that state,' she said and her cold clear voice echoed round the walls of the hall.

Math stood up, his great body towering over her and laid his staff on the ground.

'Step over that,' he ordered, 'and I shall know.'

Arianrhod bowed her head and walked towards the staff. She raised her long white skirts and lifted her foot over the king's wand. Then she dropped her skirts and gave out a long scream. Blood was running from her as she turned and fled back down the hall. The court let out a gasp of shock and surprise, for she left behind her, lying across Math's wand, a bawling newborn child with curls of yellow hair upon his head.

At a signal from Math, one of the courtiers took up the child and wrapped it in his cloak. But as Arianrhod came down the hall, she shrieked again and something else fell from her. I ran and scooped it up, covering it quickly with a scarf. Then I slipped back to my chamber and hid it in the oak chest at the foot of my bed.

After that I went back to the court. I found it deserted because Math had commanded that the child be baptized, and all had gone down to the sea. But they never brought the child back, for as soon as it felt the touch of the water, it swam across the waves and disappeared into the silvery palm of the sea-god.

While the courtiers were at the shore, I looked for Arianrhod, but could find no sign of her. So I went back to my chamber and began to weave a desperate magic over the oak chest.

Gwydion closed his eyes and began to chant, and as he did so it seemed as if the voices of the earth sang with him:

Duir, Duir, Oak of the druids,
Siniu fegub, oldest of woods.
Thou oak, bushy, leafy
Art high beyond trees.

Shritem acthe, most sacred of places,
Ergnai fith, most noble of woods,
Clothe the Land's hope
in your magical womb.

Child of the wooden womb
soul inside *Duir*,
may you grow strong of limb
like your fair mother.
Learn from the tree your art,
poet oak-birthed and wrought
mage like your father. [25]

As he intoned the words of power, I shivered. It seemed to me that with them he was entering the borders of the Unknown, seeking to command the very forces of creation. But already he had closed his eyes and was returning to his story.

When nine months had gone by, there came a cry from the chest. I opened it and there was a baby boy pushing away the folds of the scarf and trying to climb out. I wept tears of joy and hugged him to me. Then I took him to a wet nurse to be suckled.

The child grew fast and was a strong and pretty boy. At court the women doted on him and called him by all kinds of pet names, but the child as yet was nameless.

When the boy was four years old, I took him with me to Arianrhod's island. Together we dragged our little boat onto the shore and climbed the steep pathway. The boy laughed and ran through the fountains, dodging their spray, and when Arianrhod came out to greet us, he could hardly keep his eyes from her.

As we embraced I felt her stiffen in my arms. I looked at her and her eyes were dark.

I pushed the boy forward.

'Who is he?' she asked.

I drew a quick breath. I had prepared for this moment.

'Do you not know?' I said.

Her eyes flashed accusation at me.

'What have you done?' she said, 'Why have you shamed me?'

'You think it is shaming to have a boy as fine a this?' I asked.

She raised her head and speared me with her anger:

'What is your son's name?' she asked.

When I remained silent a light came into her eyes.

'Has he not been given a name?'

I shook my head.

'Then,' said Arianrhod, and something of her old power rose within her, 'he shall not receive a name until I give him one!'

With these words she turned on her heel and left us.

The boy was cowed, but my heart leaped within me. For I knew that, in spite of her great anger, she had acknowledged him.

Again the druid stopped and eyed me keenly. He began patterning the dry leaves with his hands.

'Next day,' he said, 'we set sail for the Menai Straits. There we walked beside the shore and gathered dulse and seaweed. I transformed the plants into a hide of fine soft leather.'

He began to play his harp again. As he played, I heard the lilt of the waves and saw, in my mind's eye, a small and brightly painted galleon riding them.

'Yes, that was what I conjured' said Gwydion. 'And I gave the boy and myself a dark colouring, as if we had come from the coast of Spain and brought its goods and bounty.' He continued:

We sailed back again to Arianrhod's island and dropped anchor. Then we began to stitch the leather into shoes. The ones we sent up to her were exquisite – dark red and dainty with a patterning of gold upon the toe and heel. Arianrhod was delighted and immediately sent a servant to us with her foot size. We made a pair and sent them up to her. But she returned them, saying they were too big. Then we made another pair. This time they were too small. After that I asked her to come down to the ship so that I could take her measurements myself.

Arianrhod climbed into the ship and I took her foot in my hands. I glanced towards the boy. He was holding a sling and looking intently at a tiny wren that had just alighted on the deck. He flung the stone and hit the bird neatly on the thighbone. Arianrhod clapped her hands.

'Well-aimed, Fair one of the sure hand!' she exclaimed.

I let her foot drop to the ground. At the same time, the trappings of the boat faded, as did the swarthiness of my skin and that of the boy's. We stood before her stripped of our enchantment.

'Aha!' I said. 'He is 'The Fair One of the Sure Hand', 'Lleu, Llaw Gyffes!'

Her face turned white with anger.

'So, brother, you have tricked me!' she cried. 'And the boy has found his name.'

She flashed her eyes.

'But you need not think you can outwit me so easily! Soon he will need arms, and I tell you that without his mother's blessing he shall never have them!'

Holding her head high, she climbed out of the ship and went back to her castle.

Again the boy was cowed, but again my heart leaped within me. For the boy had proved himself and earned his name.

Gwydion fell silent. I looked up and caught his eye.

'I do not expect you to understand this yet,' he said. 'How could you, with your weak knowledge of the Goddess?'

Stung by his remark, I turned my head and looked out through the trees. I heard him speak softly behind me.

'Do not feel bad,' he said. 'There are many who misunderstand her power.'

He stood up and stretched himself.

'Before we return to our story,' he said, 'there is a little tale you should know. You may think it is a silly thing, but the story has become part of our custom, and we celebrate it every year.'

He sat down again and pulled the harp towards him.

'It concerns the wren,' he said. Then he played a simple, lilting tune and sang this song:

> There was a time the birds held court
> *Ffal-a-rwdl-didl-dal*
> to choose a king was what they thought.
> *Ffal-a-rw-ho-ho*
>
> 'The king we'll have,' they said outright

Ffal-a-rwdl-didl-dal
'Should be the first in strength and might.'
Ffal-a-rw-ho-ho

The eagle raised his powerful head
Ffal-a-rwdl-didl-dal
'Then I will win!' is what he said.
Ffal-a-rw-ho-ho

'Don't be so sure,' the wren replied,
Ffal-a-rwdl-didl-dal
'for craft and cunning conquers pride.'
Ffal-a-rw-ho-ho

Then all the birds rose in the sky
Ffal-a-rwdl-didl-dal
To see how high each one could fly.
Ffal-a-rw-ho-ho

The eagle soared above them all
Ffal-a-rwdl-didl-dal
and laughed down at the wren so small.
Ffal-a-rw-ho-ho

But when he reached the highest sphere
Ffal-a-rwdl-didl-dal
He heard a squeaking in his ear.
Ffal-a-rw-ho-ho

The wren he'd carried on his wings
Ffal-a-rwdl-didl-dal
unknown to him, above him springs
Ffal-a-rw-ho-ho

He overtops the eagle's height
Ffal-a-rwdl-didl-dal
and takes the kingship with his flight.
Ffal-a-rw-ho-ho

And now the little wren doth sing
Ffal-a-rwdl-didl-dal
most lustily, for he is king.
Ffal-a-rw-ho-ho ㉖

He laid down his harp again and we laughed together.

'You must have heard that tale before,' he said.

I nodded. He looked at me and a grin crossed his face.

'It could be about me and Math,' he said.

We both began to laugh again. This time we could not stop. We roared and rolled on the ground together until the tears ran down our cheeks and our sides ached.

When we came to ourselves at last, Gwydion said: 'Actually it was about kingship.'

His face became serious.

'You know how at the turning of the year, we have the wren-hunt.'

I nodded.

'And the dead wrens are carried around the villages on a stick?'

Again I nodded, remembering how I joined in with the ritual when I was a small boy.

'That is the sacrifice of the king,' he said. 'And there is no escaping it.'

He poured some of the drink from his leather bottle.

'So now do you understand why the boy got his name from shooting at the wren?' he asked as he handed me the cup.

'Not really,' I said.

'It was his destiny to be like the wren, because he was the sacred king-child.'

He opened his pack and we ate some wheat cakes.

'Now,' said Gwydion, when we had eaten our fill. 'Are you ready to hear how he passed his second test?'

I settled down while he played another melody and the wonder of the story began to steal over me again.

After we returned home, I started to teach Lleu all the skills necessary for a young prince of the court – riding, hunting, shooting, the arts of fighting and combat, and the gentler arts of music and poetry. Then I told him to get ready for a journey.

A third time we sailed to the turning castle on Arianrhod's island. But before we arrived, I again raised an enchantment and this time turned the boy and myself into travelling bards. In this guise we came boldly up the winding path and presented ourselves at the great gate.

Arianrhod was delighted to see us, because not many bards made their way across the water to her island. We were welcomed inside and given a fine chamber for our lodging. That night, as I had done with Pryderi, I stroked my harp and told my tales, and awed all the court with my eloquence. After we retired to sleep, I slipped out and went to a lonely place to raise my magic. Then I returned to our chamber.

Next morning Lleu and I were awoken by a frenzied knocking on our door. It was Arianrhod.

'Wake up, I beg you,' she cried, 'I need your help!'

I went to the door and opened it.

'What is it? I asked.

'During the night a fleet has crept across the sea and now we are surrounded by so many ships it is impossible to see the colour of the sea between them!' she exclaimed, wringing her hands. 'Oh, help me, please, for I do not know what to do!'

'Go and fetch armour,' I commanded. 'The boy and I are both skilled in arms and will try to help you as best we can.'

She hurried to fetch two suits of armour for us.

When she returned I said, 'Lady, while I arm myself, I must ask you to arm the boy, for he has less experience.'

Without a second thought, she began to arm him. As soon as she had finished, I started to unstrap my armour. She stared at me in horror and then in growing realization as the noise of the enemy fleet subsided and the calm sweep of the empty sea encircled the island once more.

Then the enchantment fell from us both, so that she saw us plainly.

Her blazing eyes met mine, and with them, the force of our powers. Each challenge she had given him, the boy had overcome. It was the time for his third and final testing. We both knew it and we both knew that behind it lay the testing of her own power – the power of the Goddess.

She said: 'Now that through your cunning, the boy has faced an enemy and received his arms, he will soon be ready for a wife.'

The light of power flashed again from her dark eyes. She towered over Lleu, who quailed before her.

'But I lay this third and final fate upon him,' she cried. 'Never shall he enjoy the love of a mortal woman! Never shall he be wedded to a human wife!'

And with that she strode away, leaving us alone in the chamber, her cruel words still ringing in our ears.

25
Flowerbride

Annwn – the deepest land,
the Mother's gaping womb,
Annwn, the deepest land
the cradle of creation.
Held in your fastness
lies the word –
the sacred inspiration.
Druids journey there,
endure initiations and receive
your secret wisdom.
Three times has Gwydion
reached your threshold,
at the third descending
to your ancient heart [27]

It was a fresh dewy morning when we both sat again in the oak grove, the sacred place for the sacred story.

After singing his song, Gwydion put his harp aside. I knew it was not really he who had sung it, but a voice he had summoned from deep beneath the earth.

'Well?' he said, raising a bushy brow enquiringly, 'have you worked out what I did?'

'If Lleu wasn't allowed to marry a mortal woman,' I said, 'did you shape-change an animal into a woman for him?'

He laughed. 'A good guess!' he said 'and not far off.'

He unwrapped his harp.

'But we did better than that!'

He began tuning it with the little wooden key.

'Think of the role of the king,' he said, 'What is its meaning?'

He looked at me expectantly. When I hesitated he said, 'What on earth do they teach you nowadays in Druid College?'

'The king weds the land,' I said.

'That much we already know,' said Gwydion.

'He is chosen by the Goddess.'

That, too, we know,' said Gwydion.

'His role is sacred.'

'Ah!' said the druid, 'and why is that?'

'Because,' I answered, thinking wildly, 'because it involves a sacrificial death.'

Gwydion sat back.

'It is a relief to know they still teach you something of the old wisdom,' he said, 'and what is the purpose of such sacrifice?'

Again I thought wildly. It was an ancient belief, one that was no longer practised. I was struggling to remember its meaning.

'I think it's to do with fertility,' I said at last, 'and the turning of the year.'

'Good,' said Gwydion. 'But sadly I see it is no longer at the forefront of the druid teaching, even though it lies at the root of all their wisdom.'

He sighed and picked up his staff. He looked closely at the ogham symbols carved into it. Then he spoke:

'At the darkest point of the year, the sun-god dies. And when he dies everything dies with him. For without him there can be no new crops or vegetation, no warmth, no fertility, no new life.'

'But!' he continued, his grey eyes flashing, 'at the moment of death, the chasm gapes, the gates between the worlds stand open while all creation waits for the sun-god to renew himself.'

He looked deep into my eyes. 'And, of course, he does!' He paused.

'And the ritual slaying and the rebirth of the sacred king-child, holds this truth. For he is the Child of Promise, the Child of Light, and by his resurrection he can bring the earth to life once more.' He put down his staff.

'And though men have forgotten, She, the Goddess, understands this wisdom and never forgets. Remember that while I tell you the third part of my story.'

He pulled the harp-strings with his fingers and spilled a handful of music like a shower of birdsong into the air.

At first, I doubted Arianrhod. I thought she had outwitted me for the sake of wreaking vengeance and with no thought of the boy's destiny. After we returned home, I locked myself in my chamber and brooded. I took on wolf-nature and growled and snapped to myself. I also muttered spells against her, for I was determined to outwit her. But all the while a fog lay on my mind and I could see no way forward, nothing that would help the boy. For three days I brooded, plotting empty schemes and eating nothing. Then I heard footsteps, and a heavy staff banged on my door.

Gwydion picked up his staff again and began parting the dry leaves with it, exposing the moist earth.

I opened the door. It was Math. When I told him how Arianrhod had cursed the boy, his eyes burned. At first I thought that, like me, he was angry. But then I sensed that it was something else. He was excited. And his eyes burned so brightly that I felt their power travel up my spine. I saw how he relished the challenge, I saw him stride out to meet it. Power flamed round his head and the room became charged with magic while he considered what we must do.

'Of course, it will need both of us,' he said suddenly, 'but I expect she already thought of that!'

Gwydion began to scratch ogham symbols in the soil.

Then he told me what we must do. The plan was daring, it needed high magic, the full force of our combined powers. Even so, there was no certainty that we could make it work. Nevertheless we began the preparations. Math marked out ogham signs on the chamber floor and then built a fire while I went out to gather branches of oak, broom and meadowsweet. When I brought them back I began weaving them together into human shape.

For three days and nights we worked. We built a skeleton of branches, veined it with leaves and fleshed it with flowerheads and scattered petals. All the while the two of us muttered invocations to the gods, infusing the room with wood and incense smoke and calling on the powers of the elements to enter our creation.

In the dim flame-light we called on the earth to clothe her, we called up sap to flow in her, and raised a wet mist to glaze her dry-branched body. Then we called up fire to raise a passion in her, and air to lend her breath. When we had finished, we waited with beating hearts. At first nothing happened. Then, as we watched, slowly the slender figure began to fill with light. Shafts of it leaped from limb to limb as the branches thrilled into bones, the twigs and leaves into veins and sinews, and the petals smoothed into skin. With a deep shudder, the leafy casing of the lungs filled with air, and the woman opened her eyes. She stood unsteadily for a moment while the two of us stared at her in wonder, then she laughed and started walking towards us, shedding twigs and leaves all round her. When she stumbled, I reached out to catch her. I held her in my arms and heard the light patter of her heart and smelled the fragrant perfume of her skin and hair.

We called her Blodeuwedd, meaning *flowers*, because that was the essence of her. When she was brought before Lleu he thought he had never before seen a woman so wonderful, for she was perfect in every detail.

She married Lleu, and Math gave them the cantrev of Ardudwy to rule, and a fine castle to live in. They set up home there for a time and, I think, were happy. Lleu must have trusted her, for he left her alone while he went to visit Math.

But after he had gone, she became bored and restless. It was early spring, the time of blossom and bud, when sap begins to rise up from the earth. Lleu should never have left her at such a time. He should have remembered she was made out of the raw elements of nature and had the ways of the wild in her blood.

Gwydion pulled the harp towards him again and began to play a rippling melody. It spoke of the stir of the breeze over the lake and the dark stones hidden on the river-beds. When he opened his mouth, the voice of Nature herself spoke through him:

My hair is like buttermilk
And strays about my head
like soft-stringed music.
My skin is petal silk.

My arms are sinewy as sapling branches
My hands are like leaves – O like leaves
So delicately veined.

My eyes are green glass as the sea.
From the ninth wave was my being hailed
I am not of fair Cymru.

And though I laugh
and speak and move.
When you look into my green glass eyes
you see your own reflected love.

Now I walk in the world of men
Let no one give me his trust.
The sap is rising in me, O it's rising!
And I will find love where I must. ㉘

Gwydion put his harp aside and looked at me.

'So you see how it was with her,' he said simply.

One day, while Lleu was still away, Blodeuwedd looked out from the castle window and saw a flash of mottled brown and red between the trees. It was a stag, and close behind it came a hunter in fierce pursuit. She heard a crash as he brought it down and saw the trail of broken branches and the swathe of shivering leaves that marked its blundering passage. Several hours later, just as dusk was gathering, the hunter came up to the castle gates, bloodied from flaying the carcass. He asked if he might have shelter for the night and Blodeuwedd gave orders to let him in.

The man was Gronwy Pebr, lord of the neighbouring cantrev of Penllyn. When he had bathed, he came into the Great Hall. He was dressed in Lleu's shirt and breeches, for his own were stained and torn. The servants showed him to the seat opposite Blodeuwedd. Greeting her briefly, he sat down and picked up a blackened chicken thigh. He tore the meat from it with his teeth and threw the bone to his waiting hounds. In the same fashion he ate a joint of pork and three guinea-fowl. He lifted a bowl of barley-soup to his lips and tipped his head back to drink it. When he had eaten his fill, he wiped his mouth on the sleeve of Lleu's white shirt. Then he poured a goblet-full of amber wine down his throat. Blodeuwedd watched him, her pupils growing large.

While the minstrels performed their songs and the jesters told their jokes, the hunter raised his goblet and toasted his beautiful hostess. He kept his eyes on her while he emptied another goblet and yet another. The two remained drinking and toasting each other until all the musicians and servants had left the hall.

Once the hunter and the flowerbride were alone he pushed his chair back from the table and came towards her. She stood up, holding his gaze. Her look was wild, her eyes shining. He came up to her and, to his inflamed senses, it seemed as if the lips of a thousand pollen-laden flower heads were opening to him. Intoxicated, he fell towards her, and she took him in her arms.

That night he stayed in Blodeuwedd's chamber. They were in a fever of desire, gripped by the powerful onslaught of the season. Next day they went hawking together. In the evening they dined together as before and that night they made love again.

Nights and days went by and their passion flowed. Then one morning Blodeuwedd started up white-faced, for she remembered it was time for Lleu's return. The lovers clung together in an agony.

'I cannot lose you,' said the hunter,

'I will die without you,' said the flowerbride.

'Then we must kill him,' said the hunter.

'But his life is protected by a magic spell,' said Blodeuwedd.

'Even so, there will be a way,' said Gronwy, 'and you must find it.'

Then he went back to Penllyn, with Blodeuwedd's tearful promise ringing in his ears.

Later that day Lleu returned and Blodeuwedd greeted him lovingly. She came to his bed that night and began to caress him. Then suddenly she drew away.

'What is the matter?' he asked.

'I am frightened that one day you will leave me and never return,' she said.

He laughed and stroked her hair.

'How can that be when I am protected by such a great magic?' he asked.

'I had forgotten that,' said Blodeuwedd. 'What is the magic?'

'A spell that Gwydion put on me when I was in the oak chest.'

'Tell me the spell,' she said.

'Gwydion told me to keep it secret,' he replied.

'But surely not from me!'

She turned towards him and her lips trembled.

'It would mean so much to me to know how difficult it is to kill you,' she said. 'It would give me peace of mind.'

Lleu sighed. 'I can only be killed by a blow from a spear,' he said, 'but the spear must have been forged for a year and only during the time when religious rites are being performed.'

'Is that the whole spell?' asked Blodeuwedd.

'No,' he answered. 'There are a few other restrictions besides.'

'Good,' she said, kissing his chest, 'because I am still anxious for you.'

When Lleu hesitated, she brought her mouth close to his.

'Tell me!' she said.

'I can neither be killed inside or outside a house, nor on horseback or on foot!'

'Then how can you be killed?' she asked.

Lleu paused, weighing up the wisdom of telling her. At last he sighed and said: 'If a bath is placed on a river bank and half-covered with a thatched roof, and a goat is tethered beside it – then if I put one foot on the bath and the other on the goat, and raise myself up, whoever throws the spear at me then will kill me.'

Blodeuwedd laughed.

'Thank the gods for that!' she said, 'such a death can easily be avoided!'

Next day Blodeuwedd sent a message to Gronwy, and the hunter began sharpening a spear on the holy days.

Gwydion stretched himself.

'While we let a year pass,' he said, 'let us have something to eat.'

We opened our leather bags and ate some goats' cheese pressed between two flat pieces of bread. Then we gathered some blackberries and sat munching them and drinking watered wine from the druid's flask. When we had finished Gwydion settled back against the tree once more.

A year later Blodeuwedd went off into the grounds of the castle and when she returned she ran to Lleu laughing and dancing like a young girl.

'Come with me,' she cried, 'and see what I have prepared for you.' She pulled him by the hand and led him down to the Cynfael river. There he saw a thatched awning with a bath half under it, and beside the bath a tethered goat.

'Now,' she said, 'have your bath and we'll see if you really can stand with one foot on a bath and the other on a goat. Then I'll hold the goat and see if you can stay up just for a second!'

She laughed and Lleu laughed with her. She bundled him into the bath and made him wash. Then, as he raised himself naked to his feet, she helped him put one foot on its side. He slipped twice, but the third time, holding onto her, he managed to keep upright and tremblingly placed his other foot on the goat's back.

As soon as he did so, he heard a loud hiss, and a shaft of silver streaked towards him. It gashed deep into his side where its barbed point caught fast, its shaft quivering. Lleu staggered, still balanced on the bath. Then suddenly his flailing arms became covered with feathers, his legs withered into claws and his mouth puckered into a savage pointed beak. With an unearthly cry, half-human and half-animal, he lifted his wings and flew up into the sky, the spear still hanging from his side.

Gwydion stopped speaking and tears came in his eyes. When he spoke again, his voice was pained and weary:

As soon as he had got rid of Lleu, Gronwy raised an army and marched into Ardudwy. He took over the cantrev and ruled it from Lleu's palace, with Blodeuwedd at his side.

He sighed, a deep and melancholy sigh.

I tried to find him, I tried to summon him in dream. But all that came to me were images of tangled branches. Then I began to hear a noise, minute, insistent. I could hardly hear it at first, but there it was, the sound of a wing-flap, almost too faint to notice.

Fearing the worst, I set out on foot to look for him. I travelled all over Gwynedd and Powys, enquiring of everyone I met. But no one had seen Lleu or heard news of him. At last, late in the day, I came to Arvon and took lodging with a farmer.

Early next morning, I heard a loud grunting and squealing beneath my window. I looked out in time to see a great sow streaking across the fields, faster than a spear's flight. I asked the farmer's wife where the sow had gone and she said that no one knew, it ran so fast that no one could keep up with it.

That night I dreamed I was a sow again with my snout against the earth, seeking out truffles in the roots of trees. But as I nudged at them the truffles became rotten and decayed. They began to crumble away, and beneath me I saw the cave of Annwn gape open. Then I awoke and the vision left me

Next morning I got up very early and waited beside the sty. As soon as the sow was released I went with her. With the speed of the wind in fury, we hurled ourselves through valleys, over hills, across far-spreading fields. The landscaped changed about us as we flew, the valleys filled with purple, the hilltops streaked with silver and the moorland turned pale gold before us. At last, we wove between the tangled branches of a forest and came out on a vast silver plain with a huge oak tree standing in the middle, its great arms stretching to the skies. The sow rushed towards the tree and suddenly stopped, her great sides heaving, and began snuffling at its roots. I took back my own form and looked down at her. I saw that, instead of finding truffles, she was gorging on decaying flesh. I looked up. The tree was thickly branched and endless, its crown lost among the clouds. Whatever was perched at the top of it was hidden from sight. But as I looked, the noise of wing-flaps beat furiously inside my ears and my heart began to flare and pound.

Then I knew that I had come to the very axis of the world, the mystic pillar reaching from the gates of Annwn to the realms of the sky god. I was at the meeting point between gods and men, between earth and spirit. I stood beneath the World Tree and high above me, I knew that Lleu was hanging on its branches.

As I marvelled, the wing-flaps beat louder and more furiously in my ears. The tree was trembling with the force of it. Its pulse was so strong I stumbled away and sat on the silver grass of the plain. Then I spoke my ritual and went into spirit.

Straightaway I was taken to the abyss beneath the Poet's Seat at Arianrhod's Castle. From its depths a voice was calling to me. It was Lleu. At the sound of his urgent cries, I leaped into the darkness. I was falling between dark cliffs with nothing but the wind around me and nothing below me but the realms of the Unknown.

Gwydion opened his eyes and gripped his staff.

'I descended into the womb of the Mother. It was the deepest place below the earth, the very cradle of creation.' His voice fell to a whisper. 'There I found the *awen*.' As he spoke, his face was shining.

'It is not for me to speak of it,' he said. 'Such things each man must discover for himself.'

'When I came back, I had in my head the words of an *englyn*, a song of power. I sat beside the World Tree and began to sing it.'

Gwydion picked up his harp and began chanting to an ancient plaintive melody:

> Grows an oak between two lakes,
> darkly shadowed sky and glen.
> If I do not speak untruth
> these are petals from Lleu's fair flowers.

As I sang, the trembling of the tree grew stronger, I felt it shivering in its topmost branches. I looked up and, breaking through the clouds, I saw the form of an eagle half-fluttering, half-falling to the branches below. I sang another verse:

> Grows an oak on upland plain,
> nor rain wets it nor heat melts.
> Nine score hardships hath he felt.
> In its top Lleu Llaw Gyffes.

Again I stopped and looked up into the tree. High above me I saw the eagle slowly shifting and falling down its branches. Then I sang a third verse:

Grows an oak upon a steep
sanctuary of a fine fair lord.
If I do not speak untruth
Lleu will come into my lap. ㉙

When I had finished singing the eagle fluttered from the lowest branch and into my lap. Straightaway I struck it with my staff. At once its feathers fell away, its beak uncurled, its legs stretched and strengthened, its claws formed into feet, and its wings into arms and hands. It was Lleu. But he was a piteous sight, little more than skin and bone.

I carried him back to Math's palace where I tended him with herbs and medicines and with my magic arts. It took a full year to bring him back. At first, he was too weak to speak of what had happened, but gradually his power returned to him, and at last he felt strong enough to join our counsel.

Math and I had been debating how to punish Gronwy and Blodeuwedd. When Lleu joined us, I told him that, as her maker, I wanted to deal with Blodeuwedd myself. Lleu agreed to leave her fate to me, but said he wanted to challenge Gronwy, the man who had taken his wife, his castle and his lands. Over the next few weeks we made our plans and, as soon as Lleu was fit enough, Math mustered his troops and we set out for Ardudwy.

After many days' journey we reached Lleu's castle and found it deserted. Word of our coming had gone ahead and Gronwy had fled to the forest while Blodeuwedd and her maidens had escaped to the mountains. Lleu and Math went to the forest in search of

Gronwy, and I headed for the mountains.

Blodeuwedd's maidens had run on ahead of her. But such was their fear that they kept looking backwards and fell into a lake. As I came after Bodeuwedd I passed their floating bodies. Then I saw Blodeuwedd. She was standing waiting for me, and there was no fear in her eyes. I came up to her and cursed her. I told her death was too good for her and that I would turn her into a bird. In answer, she gave me a strange smile. Then I said:

'But you shall become a bird of night, the most hated bird of all, the bird that is mobbed by all the other birds.'

At this, she threw back her head and began to laugh. As she laughed, I raised my wand in fury and spoke the words of power. I struck her with it and her lips pushed forward, snapping into hardness, her eyes grew rounded and her pupils yellow-orbed. Feathers sprang from her cheeks and her downy arms curved into wings. But all the while, her laughter came in shrieking hoots. At last, when the transformation was complete, she sprang from the ground and, for a brief moment, stretched her talons towards my eyes. Then she soared triumphantly above me and disappeared into the sky.

Gwydion caught the look of surprise in my eyes and held up his hand, motioning me to hold my questions until the story had ended.

As for Gronwy, Lleu soon caught him. He took him to the Cynvael River, to the very spot where he himself had been speared. The hunter pleaded with him. He said: 'Lord, since it was by the wiles of a woman that I tried to kill you, in the name of the gods will you show me a little mercy. Let me hold a stone between myself and the blow.'

Lleu agreed to that, so Gronwy set a great stone in front of him.

While the hunter waited behind the stone, Lleu ascended the hill and lifted his spear. It was his own spear, a spear of unerring aim, a spear that always found its mark. Lleu hurled it with all the strength he had and the magic weapon pierced right through the stone and deep into Gronwy's cowering body.

And after that Lleu went back to his palace and reigned over his people once more and there was great joy at his return.

Gwydion stood up stiffly.

'The stone still stands beside the river,' he said. 'One day I will take you there and show it to you. It has a great hole where Lleu's spear went through it.'

He took a drink from the bottle and offered it to me.

'Of course, I didn't understand everything then,' he said, when we had finished drinking. 'I was a player in the story, caught up in the vengeance and the emotion of it, unable to see the whole picture. I know better now.' He clapped me on the back. 'And, of course, it's all to do with the Goddess!'

He chuckled. 'She used me,' he said, 'I was her tool. I did her bidding even when I thought I had outwitted her. Even when I made the flowerbride – in fact, *especially* then!'

Seeing my bewilderment grow even greater, he said: 'But I don't suppose you'll understand until you hear it from her yourself.'

'What do you mean?' I asked.

'It is not for me to speak for her. The three of them must speak their mysteries themselves.'

'How?' I asked.

'Make yourself ready and we'll summon them,' he replied.

We built up the fire and while it grew in strength, went out from the sacred grove and gathered symbols of the seasons, a fir cone, a young plant, a cluster of berries, and a dry leaf. Gwydion made a circle and I brought in the delicate gifts, placing them to face the four directions. Then, taking some earth and sprinkling it with water, he moulded it into the form of a woman. After that he took a branch still smouldering from the fire and smudged the figure with its smoke. Raising his staff over it, he called on the Three-fold Goddess of the Land to show herself.

I do not know how long we waited, stilling our minds and conjuring shapes but I do remember that at last the smoke fanned out into a cloud. After that it seemed we were in an altered place in which the sounds of birds and animals were stilled and we were surrounded by a mist, which spread out in a huge circle around us. The mist shook and thickened and seemed to be twisting into a storm cloud. Then suddenly, striking through the cloud, came a shaft of light, so bright we had to shut our eyes. When we opened them again we saw a shape forming itself out of the misty brightness. It was a woman standing in silhouette beside a tree. The outline of her breasts was clearly visible. But as she turned to face us, her breasts appeared in silhouette again. Then she advanced towards us, while a second shape waited on the horizon.

As she drew near we could see she had yellow hair that flowed down her back, a face pale as the moon, and wide, staring eyes. She bowed her head stiffly as if greeting Gwydion, then she looked at me, at least she seemed to, but her gaze went through me and beyond. After that she spoke and her voice came and went like delicate sparks of sunlight flickering on little waves.

I, Goewin, am Virgin footholder to Math the King. It is I who guard his feet. They rest in my lap for I am Sovereignty and guard the land, and he is king of it. When the time is ready, Gwydion will turn the wheel so I become woman. Then the King must wed me. After the marriage I am Modron, the Mother who prepares for the birth of Mabon, the sacred child. Listen and understand this mystery.

The delicate, beautiful figure faded and at once the second shape came forward, dark-haired and with a wheel of silver stars about her. She, too, looked both through me and beyond. Then she spoke and her voice was strong and proud like the leaping of bright flames:

I, Arianrhod, am Virgin Goddess in Caer Sidi. Called by the King, and tried by his potent staff, I birth the Divine child, the Mabon. Then I become the Challenger for there are three tests that the child must pass.

First he must learn his name, for in it lies his destiny. He is the King of birds, the little wren, whose fate is to be hunted down and killed.

Second, he must learn the skills of war and earn his arms. Surrounded by enemies he must show no fear. Only by passing such a test, can he be armed.

And third, he is fated never to marry mortal woman. For, once he is king, only the land can be his bride.

Listen and understand this mystery.

With these last words, the proud figure turned and walked away.

Then it seemed as if the young tree itself came forward. As it drew near, I saw the face of Blodeuwedd lifting from a halo of leaves.

She spoke in a voice of wind and water:

I, Blodeuwedd, am young as the newborn tender reed and old as the hoary mountain. Through me the seasons pass. I am Virginity, the birth of spring, I am full-bodied summer when ripe corn stands in the fields, I am the thresher when the autumn comes. In winter I embrace the bare-branched trees and bring forth death. Wedded to the King it is I who command his sacrifice and his renewal. Then I become the Wise One. Listen and understand. For with the turning of the year I come again, renewed.

Then she, too, left us. As she went the light within the grove faded and we found ourselves in near-darkness.

'You see,' Gwydion's voice came softly, 'that is how it is. Do you now understand a little?'

26
The Song of the Shaman

It was our last day in the sacred grove. The next morning we were to move on from the village.

After we had been sitting for a while in silence, Gwydion looked at me intently.

'Remember my story,' he said. 'Remember how I learned my bardic craft and held the hearts of all who listened to my singing. Remember how I learned the seer's arts, by raising great illusions with my magic, and taking on the natures of wild beasts. And remember how I used the druid's power of *awen* and raised up the sacred king-child from the dead. Remember these things if you remember nothing else.'

He picked up his harp. 'As it happens,' he said, 'I have made a song of it.'

Then he began to sing:

Twice-birthed, and rising through the waters of the spirit
Otherworlds have claimed me.
In the deep cauldron have I three times forged my
 changing,
In the deep cauldron have I three times changed shape.

Shape of the stag has been my covering
and I have shivered in the fold of winter branches,

fought horn to horn and bellowed on the mountainside,
fought horn to horn and roared on the hill.

Then entering the sow, I learned its nature
snuffling out truffles, suckling my young
and seeking out nourishment in lowly places,
seeking out nourishment under the ground.

And after these changes, wolf's wildness seized me,
Running with the wolf pack, by night and by day,
Howling at the moon and playing the predator,
Howling at the moon and seizing my prey.

So have I served my training from bard into druid
From harper to shaman, from seer into sage.
Long has been the journey through the halls of dark wisdom,
hard the transforming from trickster to mage.

First I was bard and spun my bold stories,
trying out my tricks and overcoming kings.
Then I endured my many changes in the cauldron
Taking the shape of wild beasts as I've told.

Last the high magic of the druid
conjured from the power of song and of word
and restoring to life – the highest of wisdoms,
restoring to life, the greatest good. ㉚

When he had finished singing, he looked at me again.

'I asked for a companion to record my wisdom,' he said, 'for soon it will be time for me to pass into spirit.'

He pressed my hand.

'Do not be grieved, for another will come. He will be known as the Child of the Shining Brow. I know of his coming for I have seen him already. His name is Taliesin and he will be born of the wisdom of the Great Cauldron.'

He smiled at me.

'Tonight I will be telling the story of Taliesin's birth to the villagers. So you can hear one of my famous bardic performances for yourself! I have honed the story over the years and, although my fingers are not as nimble as they once were, I can still accompany the great bard's poems prettily enough.'

When he saw my eyes fill with tears, he laid his arm on my shoulder.

'These are hard mysteries,' he said, 'and it is difficult to speak of them. But you must understand that as I look forward to the wisdom of Taliesin, so, when he comes, he will look back to mine. Our wisdoms will become one and thus the flame of truth, the essence of our being, will live forever.'

He pressed my hand again. His eyes were shining.

'It will be the same for you' he said, 'when your time comes.'

27
Taliesin, the Shining Child

Gwydion came down to the village at dusk. He stood in the half light before the newly-burning fire and raised his arms while the smoke wreathed behind him. Then, lifting up his voice, he began to intone a prayer to the goddess. 'Oh, Ceridwen, great queen,' he cried, 'goddess of life and death, yours is the sacred white sow who gleams with the pearls of the night, who scents out the earthy pathways to the Otherworld. Mountain Mother, Cailleach, Ancient Wise One, yours is the great cauldron, sacred womb and vessel of transformation. For in your cauldron lies the brew which conjures wisdom, in your cauldron lies the brew which wakens inspiration, in your cauldron lies the brew which lifts the spirit into life!'

Then, as the fire flared up and lit our faces, striking a low chord on his harp he began to tell his tale:

The great goddess Ceridwen, mightier than a mountain, wiser than the wiliest of serpents, older than time itself, lived in a house with her husband Tegid Voel. Their house rose up on stilts from the middle of a great lake, Lake Tegid in North Wales, so that it seemed as if it floated upon the waters. And from the house at all times arose a great mist, for the goddess was a witch and spent her time conjuring powerful brews in the depths of her sacred cauldron which she kept in a dark and secret chamber.

A day came when the great goddess conceived a child. And because she herself was night and day, death and life, darkness and light, wizened yet beautiful, the child lay in the womb and thought what it would be. Then the child chose and pulled the dark out of his mother, winding it about him like a shroud from the heavens, like a ribbon from a well of black water, like the damp, velvet breath in the belly of the deepest cave beneath the earth. As soon as the child was born Ceridwen saw that it had wrapped itself in the cloak of night so she named the boy Morfra, which means The Great Crow. And the boy-child grew up with a lowered brow and a hunched shoulder and became so misshapen that Ceridwen renamed him and gave him the blackest name of all: Avagddu, which means 'Utter Darkness'.

Then Ceridwen conceived again and, this time, as the child lay in the womb with the waters around it, she did not feel the dark below her with its mysterious profundity but only the dance of the sunlight endlessly spiralling on its surface, the pull of the waves lifting and reaching towards the light. So the child smiled in the dream world of its forming and chose the brightness. And when it was born Ceridwen saw the golden streaks of hair still gleaming on its shoulders and the ringlets standing on its head like curls of yellow sunlight and she called her Creirwy, which means 'Dear One'. And the girl-child grew up dear indeed, for it seemed that she had the sun itself by the tail, and everywhere she went she brought radiance and light, brightness and laughter, delight and joy.

Her dark and bright children were as night and day, woe and joy, death and life to Ceridwen. But she knew that out of the darkness comes the understanding of secret knowledge, and that deep in the cave beneath the mountain lies the tiny seed of inspiration. So when she went to prepare her magic brew, it was not for the bright child Creirwy that she brewed it, but for her dark one, Avagddu, so that he might have the vision that comes out of the darkness, and the wisdom that is found in the dreams of the night.

So she consulted the Books of the Fferyllt, the ancient books of magic, turning their fragile pages and reading the faded letters of the spells. Then she went to the dark chamber where the great cauldron lay. As she opened the casement window onto the night, in came a shiver of light from the moon. It struck the row of white pearls that beaded the great rim and ran silver lines around the ogham symbols etched into its great black bowl. Then Ceridwen put fresh white candles into the four great silver candlesticks around the cauldron and lit them with a taper. Kneeling before the cauldron, she raised her great arms towards it and spoke this incantation:

Tongues from the fire of inspiration,
Drops from the waters of wisdom
Stones from the bony dwellings of the earth
Smoke from the scented places of the air
mingle in this brew.
And from the potent waters
of the womb of greatness,
bring to birth the *awen* –
gift of deepest wisdom,
deepest knowing,
deepest inspiration.

And the cauldron echoed with her chanting, it rang and sang in its hollow emptiness and waited for its magic belly to be filled. Then Ceridwen began to prepare a potent brew, a brew that would confer on her son the three gifts of knowledge, wisdom and inspiration. She went out at night and gathered herbs, she set traps and caught small creatures, skinning them and adding their skeletons to the potion. Then she stripped the barks from trees and crushed their sap, and pounded to dust the dark-faced jewels of opal and amethyst. Every night she added these ingredients and every time she was careful to speak the correct spells and incantations. When, at last, the brew was ready, the cauldron was to be stirred and kept boiling for a year and a day, and for this Ceridwen appointed Morden, a blind old man. He came to her accompanied by the young boy who led and guided him, whose name was Gwion Bach.

The old man with Gwion Bach at his side, faithfully kept the pot boiling for a whole year and never ceased from stirring it, while Ceridwen attended to her other duties. But just one day before its final distillation was complete, the three magic drops, impatient to be in the world, jumped out and landed on the thumb of the young boy. The pain set his eyes pricking and he put his thumb in his mouth to ease it.

At once his eyes became as big as platters – for, in an instant, he became possessed of all knowledge, wisdom and inspiration. He saw to the edges of the world and beyond, he saw into the fastnesses of the history of the world and of man, and he saw into the shining places where the silver darting fish of inspiration lie just out of sight. All such things he saw, these being the properties of the three drops. Then the fear of Ceridwen came on him for he knew, even without the inspired knowledge that was in him, that she would kill him because he had stolen the essence of her brew. So he ran from the place as fast as he could, hoping to gain ground before Ceridwen discovered what had happened.

Meanwhile the cauldron cracked open with a great cry and the remaining brew flowed out of it and away down the hill and into a stream where the horses of king Gwyddno drank of it and were poisoned.

When Ceridwen realized what had happened and how her son was cheated of his potion, she set out after Gwion Bach in a great rage. But Gwion had new powers so he dropped his arms to the ground. At once his skin turned soft and grey, his long ears streamed back, and the grass streaked past as he became a hare and ran for his freedom across the fields.

But Ceridwen turned herself into a black greyhound and soon he heard her growling and snapping behind him. He reached a river and, jumping in, took fish-nature, twisting and turning and breasting the current. But, otter-formed, Ceridwen dived after him. Then he leaped into the air and stretched his two fins wider and wider until they became two feathered wings, and with them he flew over hill and valley seeking his escape. But the goddess took hawk-form and followed him with her bright eyes and powerful wings until she came close enough to swoop on him. Then he changed into the smallest form of life he knew, dropping to the earth as a grain of wheat and lying still and quiet on the farmyard floor. But Ceridwen had seen him. Alighting on the ground, she became a strutting black, red-crested hen and, in one swift movement, bent her beak to the floor and pecked him up.

After this she transformed herself back into human shape. But the grain was still inside her. It swelled and grew with the light of the favoured child, and nine months later she gave birth to a baby boy. But when she looked at him, she saw that the child's face shone so brightly that she was unable to harm him. So she put him in a leather bag and sent him out to sea in a coracle.

There the child lay with the star-glow of knowledge, wisdom and inspiration within him, riding lightly on the waves, biding his time. Long days and nights he lay in the coracle, rocked and tossed by the waters, woken by the pink sun, while the rain fell on him and the sun dried him again, and he was made to endure and receive and wait.

Now, while the child was still rocking on the waves, a king's son was fishing for a catch of salmon. He was Prince Elphin, son of King Gwyddno. Elphin had recently amassed so many debts that his father had summoned him to his presence and given him a piece of his mind. But afterwards, because he was really very fond of his son, his father relented and decided to give his son the annual salmon catch as a chance to redeem his loss. In return Elphin had promised faithfully never to get into such straits again. But already it seemed his luck was out, for, though he had already waited for several hours, not a salmon was to be had and the nets were bare. All that pulled on them was a weed-covered coracle, tangled in a corner.

With a sigh Elphin waded into the river and carefully unhooked the coracle, and was about to throw it back into the river, when he noticed a bundle inside. He took it out and began to unwrap it. Then he felt the bundle move and soon he uncovered a child's face which glowed with such brightness that for a moment he was blinded. The child opened its eyes and in their depths he saw the turning of the planets and the whirling of the stars, the dance of the sun and the gleam in the darkest depths of the ocean. It was then the child spoke:

I am Taliesin
and the inspiration of my song
is discovered in the depths.
I know where the wave flows
into the cup, where the dawn
has its end, where the river
disappears, and where the sky
meets the earth.

I know why sadness
is better than joy
why the harpstring
laments, why the cuckoo
is sad, and the crow
is wax-coloured.

I know why a hill echoes,
why milk is white
and holly green
why the alder is purple
and why the sun is red,
I know a name of two words
which rest in the cauldron.
I know all the craft of Gwydion. (31)

And there was more, far more that the child sang as Elphin carried him over the hill and back to the palace. But the child was silent in its bag when the king asked his son about his catch.

'I haven't caught a single salmon,' said the prince, his own face radiant, 'but instead I have caught something rare indeed.'

'And what, might I ask, is that?' replied the king angrily.

'A poet,' said Elphin, handing the child to the king before he could react. As the king looked, the child opened his eyes and spoke again.

I am Taliesin,
primary chief bard.
I know why the cow has horns
and the goat a beard
why the doe is dappled
and the sea tastes salt.
And I know the foundation
that is under the sea.

I know why night comes,
and why a woman
moves with the tides,
why berries are red
and the linnet green.
I know the ways of the boar
and the tracks of the deer.

For I have been a blue salmon,
a dog, a deer

a goat on the mountain,
the trunk of a tree,
an axe in a man's hand
a pin between tongs.
A stallion, a bull
a yellow goat.

And I have been a grain
discovered. A red hen
took me up,
and I was nine months
in her womb.
I have been dead
I have been alive
I have suffered great pain
I am Taliesin.

As the child sang, the king was carried in spirit through the vastness of the universe, the great dome of the air, and the caverns of the sea. And when the child had finished and he came to himself again, the king commanded that he be brought up at court with all honours. So Taliesin was put into the care of Elphin and his wife.

Several years went by and in that time the power and magic of the boy grew stronger. When Taliesin was thirteen, Elphin went to visit his uncle Maelgwn. While there he heard Maelgwn's men praising the wisdom of his bards. Elphin boasted that his own bard, though yet a boy, could easily outstrip them all. His boast so angered Maelgwn that he ordered Elphin to be placed in the palace dungeons and chained with a silver chain. Then he sent for Taliesin, and invited him to attend a contest with the other bards.

When Taliesin arrived at court he looked for all the world like an innocent young child. Unnoticed he slipped into a dark corner of the hall and began playing with his finger on his lips making a babbling sound. He kept this up as the bards processed past him into the room. As each of them bowed to their lord and opened their mouths to praise him, they were astonished to find that nothing but the babbling sound 'blerm, blerm' would come from their lips. Outraged at their insulting noises, Maelgwn struck the chief bard Heinen with his staff. The blow broke the enchantment so that Heinen was able to speak. He told Maelgwn that his bards had been affected by the power of a spirit which had taken child-form and was sitting in the corner. Immediately Taliesin was brought before Maelgwn who looked him up and down and asked who he was. Taliesin answered:

Primary chief bard am I
to my lord Elphin
I come from the land
of Summer stars.

Merlin have I been called
but Taliesin is the name
by which kings will know me.

Nine months I waited
in Ceridwen's womb
Gwion was I once
but now am Taliesin.

I can name the stars
from North to South
and I was in Lys Don
before Gwydion
the bard was born.

Three times have I lingered
in the prison of Arianrhod
and I received *awen*
from Ceridwen's cauldron.

I have been a harper
to Deon of Lochlin
and I have starved
in service of the Mabon.

I have taken the poet's seat
at the castle of Caer Sidi,
the turning throne
between the elements.

Before all things I was
and know their history.
All the world's wonders
I, Taliesin, can reveal.

Then the boy bard addressed the wizards grouped about him saying:

You with minds of little understanding
hear one who proves his powers
in magic song and divination
seeking to release his lord,
a man confined in prison.

For the championship
of the Chair of Deganwy
I contend with strength
numbering my songs
above three hundred.
Let the ignorant bard
forfeit both jewel and ring
even the bright shield.
For I am Taliesin
and will bring my lord
from his silver chains.

If you bards are versed
in inspiration
cease quarrelling
in your king's court.
And if you are ignorant
of the forms of verse
keep silent, Heinen.
For the name of *rimiad*
and that of *ramiad*,

and who was father to you
in this mystery,
you do not know.

Begone false bards
for my lord Elphin lies below
imprisoned falsely.
You can neither sing
the song I carry
nor can you discern
truth from falsehood.
Why not depart
and go your ways
for none of you
can silence me
before death comes.

But if any hear me
let the Spirit hearken to him.

And as he sang these words a great wind rose up and buffeted the castle so that it swayed on its foundations. This caused so much alarm that the king sent immediately for Elphin to be released from prison. But Taliesin sang another verse, which caused Elphin's chains to fall from him of their own accord. Taliesin sang two more songs in rebuke of the bards, putting them all to shame. And, when he had finished, Elphin lifted up the Shining Child and carried him home.

'Look again,' said the druid, his voice softly breaking from the story, 'listen with the ears of understanding, and learn anew, for the wisdom of Taliesin is all around you. It is in the vastness of the sea, the splendour of the stars at night, and the darkness underneath the earth. It is the wisdom of time and no time, of birth and rebirth. For Taliesin is the child who has ridden on the waters of creation, been reborn of the spirit, and who shines with the great light that is within us all!'

Then he laid his fingers on his harp and, in the glow of the fire, plucked a shimmering music from its strings that sparkled like tiny jewels in our ears.

ARMORICA

ARMORICA WAS THE CELTIC NAME FOR BRITTANY AND MEANS 'THOSE LIVING BY THE SEA.'

ALTHOUGH THERE ARE NO EXTANT MEDIAEVAL TEXTS OF THEIR STORIES, THE BRETON LEGENDS HAVE BEEN HANDED DOWN ORALLY AND HAVE AN ANCIENT HERITAGE. MANY OF THEIR STORIES CONCERN THE CONFLICT BETWEEN THE EARLY SAINTS AND THE REMAINING DRUIDS AT THE TIME WHEN CHRISTIANITY CAME TO BRITTANY. THE FOLLOWING STORY IS PERHAPS THE MOST WELL-KNOWN AND IS FOUND IN THE *BARZAZ BREIZ* OR 'SONGS OF BRITTANY' COLLECTED BY VISCOUNT HERSART DE LA VILLEMARQUE IN 1838.

28
The City of Ys

I was out climbing on the rocks near the water when I saw an old woman with long black hair getting out of a boat that had landed on our shore. Although she was old and thin, she seemed brown and strong because I could see the muscle-shapes in her arms. She beckoned to me to come up close, and then bent down and made me look into her eyes. I was frightened but I looked. Her eyes were like the sky and the sea together, all grey and green and blue. It was like looking into the deep parts of the sea or to a far-away time long ago. When I had finished looking, she touched my hand and called me a star-child. 'Star-child', she said, 'Listen to my tale and remember it well.' Then she came slowly over the stones until she found a flat rock, the farthest one in from the sea, where the grass begins. She sat on it and rocked with her eyes closed and began to make some dreamy singing. Her singing filled the whole air. First it pulled on the low clouds across the water, then it hummed into the shore. It was all around and far away and it stretched on and on. It made me think of sad things, like people dying.

Soon there were people all around us coming from the village drawn by the sound. When they saw her some of them crossed themselves and turned away quickly but some just waited. Although they waited a long time, the singing made them forget all about time and about the things they should be doing. They seemed to be under a spell, and the old woman kept weaving it until it was tight as tight and we were all caught fast.

Then she opened her eyes and began to speak:

I come from our little island. It is not far off. Can you hear our Mother's tongue licking at our rocks and shingle? Can you hear her sucking out our caves? And can you see her breath, misting our shores and hiding our mysteries? One day, you will all come to us, borne white as foam across the water, and then the nine of us will stretch out our hands to you and catch your souls. But you needn't be afraid for we shall look after them.

Of course you know that *she* came. Long years ago. She came crying to us when you forsook the old ways. She still cries sometimes now, underneath the water, and some of you have heard her. But I remember when she lived on land. Listen while I tell you her story, for she is important to you.

Then, half-singing and half-chanting, the old woman began her story:

> Pale as the moon on water was her skin,
> black as the sea-washed rocks, her hair,
> while her eyes were two green fires.

When she was a girl her father worshipped her. He was the King and she the Princess. Her beautiful mother had long gone, slipping back into the sea from whence she came - so some said. And as for her father, his name was Gradlon – Gradlon the Great, and he ruled over this country of Cornouaille.

But you know this and you remember him. Yet why are you

silent about his daughter? Why is she shunned, like we, the old ones? For she sings round these shores and she sings in your head the old songs that you can never forget. And though you call her Mary Morgan, remember that her real name was Dahut. Dahut-Ahes.

They were happy together, Dahut and her father, until there came a day when Gradlon decided to go out hunting with his men in the forest of Menez-hom, some two-days' ride north of the palace. At first, the king and his men occupied themselves in hunting boar and other small game, but then they sighted a white deer and excitedly gave chase. They pursued it all through the day and into the evening until, as is the way with such creatures, it led them deep into the heart of the forest and then disappeared. By this time, night had fallen and they were far from home.

They looked about them and saw far-off a beam of light shining between the trees. They went towards it and came upon a hermit's cell, streaming with candlelight. The hermit, Corentin, came out to greet them and offered them hospitality, which they gladly accepted. Then, just as the men were making themselves comfortable, Corentin beckoned to the King to follow him. The hermit led him deeper into the forest until they came to a clearing. In the middle of it, surrounded by rich green grass, was an ancient stone well. The hermit went up close to it and held up his candle. As soon as its light fell on the black surface of the water, he began to sing an incantation:

Brother fish, little brother fish
deep in your water hollow,
Ancient Wise One come to us
for we have need of you!

At this a bright silver fish speckled with red, jumped from the well and landed at the hermit's feet. Swiftly the hermit caught it up and slit it in half with a silver knife. Then he threw half back into the well, but Gradlon saw to his amazement that the minute it touched the water it became whole again. Then Corentin took the other half of the fish back to his cell and began to cook it. A short while later the men were astonished to find that a rich feast had been made ready for them. Gradlon demanded to know how this miracle had come about. Corentin answered him:

> The well is a holy well,
> the fish is a miraculous fish
> and the food before you is the food of God.

Then Gradlon begged Corentin to return with him to the city of Quimper and become its Bishop. But the old man shook his head while tears came into his eyes. 'I hope it is not God's will that I should do that,' he said, 'for it is here that I have made my home, and here that I feel close to God.' But Gradlon pressed him, and the old man wept bitterly because he knew the time had come for him to leave. So, next morning, he packed his few belongings and went with Gradlon and his men to live in the city. But when he entered the palace, he and Dahut exchanged glances, and it was like one heart crying to another and finding no answer.

After Corentin was made bishop he hardened his heart against Dahut. For she was a wild child and liked nothing better than to run barefoot on the grassy plains and wade into the muddy rivers. She also plucked herbs and hedge flowers and discovered their healing properties. Then Corentin, who in his deepest heart pined for his old wooded haunt, began to order Gradlon to build churches to the glory of his God. More and more churches were built until, not only every town, but every village had its own temple to the Christian God. Then, at last, Corentin was satisfied.

But, as the churches grew in number, Dahut began to sicken. Her pale face became thin and sharp and her eyes lost their brightness. One day she came to her father and said: 'Father, I am dying. Now that the churches have covered the land there is no joy. The people don't dance or sing anymore, for all dancing and singing are banned.'

Then she covered her face with her hands and cried bitterly.

Gradlon was shocked. He had not realized how ill his daughter had become, and he was terrified of losing her. He promised he would give her anything if only it would save her and make her happy again. Then she raised her head and said: 'There is one thing. I long for the sea. I pine for it day and night. Build me a city beside the waves. Then I can live there and be well again.'

So her father commanded the finest builders in the land to begin construction of the greatest city that had ever been made. They laid the foundations far out on the westernmost Point du Raz. Soon the streets and avenues appeared, then courtyards with marble fountains, then mansions, fine houses with exotic gardens, palaces with gold-capped towers and cupolas that flashed in the sun by day and mirrored the moon by night. And when the fair city was finished, its slender towers speared the sky and probed into the depths of the sea, where it hung in illusion.

As the city took shape, so the roundedness came back to Dahut's breasts and the fire to her eyes. She went to live in the city with her father, and they called the city Ys. And, for a while, all was right again between father and daughter. Then one day Bishop Corentin came to visit the city. He was taken round the avenues and squares and shown the fountains and the exotic gardens, the towers and gold-capped cupolas. He saw how they flashed like rubies by day and shone like the pearls of the moon by night. He saw all this and he became white with anger. He confronted Gradlon: 'I have toured this city from north to south and from east to west,' he thundered. 'I have gone round its walls and seen every house, every garden and every street of it. But nowhere in the whole of this costly city have I found a single church!'

Gradlon was appalled at these words. He suddenly realized that, in his concern for Dahut, he had entirely forgotten the new God. Quaking before the wrath of the Bishop he promised he would give orders for a church to be built immediately.

That night Dahut came to her father wringing her hands in grief. She said she did not want a church in her city. She said that churches made her ill. She asked her father if it would please him to see her grow pale as a ghost again. She begged and implored him and used every female wile she possessed, but it was all to no avail. Gradlon said he had given Corentin his word and could not take it back.

It was then that Dahut came to us. She set out at night under a sharp moon. Pushing her little coracle from the shore she braved the black waters of the Bay of the Dead. Then, trusting to our Mother's breath to carry her, she played her small harp to soothe the ghosts and water-spirits of the place. And so she reached our island unharmed, beached her boat and came looking for us in the darkness of the woods.

She found us in the firelight, tending the Shrouded Ones. Our eyes met hers and we knew her for our own. With tears she told us her story and begged us for our Mother's sake to stop the building of the church and save her city from the new religion. Then we spoke with her about the old ways and she thought of her own mother who had left her with an aching in her heart. And then she cried a little while we tried to comfort her. At last we said that, although we could not stop the building of the church, we'd send our elves, the Korrigans, to build a castle that would tower above it and protect her. She said she also feared the rising waters of the sea and asked if the Korrigans could build a dyke to keep her city safe.

The druidess looked up then, breaking her story.

'All this was done,' she said, 'and yet the danger for Dahut lay not in the church or even in the sea, but in the very castle of her heart where she was wounded. But as to the rest of the tale, I must warn you that Dahut grows dark within it, for her goddess powers were feared and it suited the new faith to blacken her name. Remember that while I continue.'

Then she settled herself more comfortably upon the rock, and went on with her story.

Once the grand new castle was built, Dahut moved into it with her father. By now news of the great city had travelled far and wide, as had the fame of the darkly beautiful princess who held court there. Because she was now of age, countless young men and princes set out to visit her. And this, so it is said, is how she treated them. She held great feasts and dances in the castle, hiring the best cooks, bards, tumblers and musicians in the land. To these great feasts her suitors were invited. But when the feasting was ended, the one she favoured would be masked by a black-robed servant and led down a labyrinth of corridors to her chamber in the heart of the castle. There she would have her will of him. But afterwards he would be throttled by a spring inside the mask, and his body hurled into the choking torrent that raged beneath the castle.

But, if this is true, the king said nothing of it. Perhaps he simply turned a blind eye and kept to his own wing of the castle. Certainly he had the church built, but soon it fell into rack and ruin for no one attended it. And, although Gradlon saw less of Dahut, he knew she had not forgotten him, for she entrusted him with the golden key to the dyke. He wore it round his neck at all times, keeping the city safe.

Meanwhile, word that the church was ruined and neglected reached Corentin, who alerted the Abbot Guénolé. The abbot took it upon himself to go to Ys in person, and was so shocked by the godlessness of the city that he began preaching in the streets dressed in his robes and mitre, but no one listened to him. Nevertheless, he began to speak the daily rites and offices in the church.

It was about this time, that a new suitor arrived at Dahut's castle. He was dressed from head to foot in wild red silk and, when the feast began, instead of sitting down to eat, he began to dance. Slowly and sinuously he danced at first, coiling and uncoiling like a snake, then he moved faster and faster until he was spinning like a thin red pole. Dahut was spellbound by him. When at last he stopped, she begged him to come to her, but he refused.

'There's only one way you can have me,' he told her.

'What is that?' she asked.

'If you get the key that opens the sluice-gate of the dyke, and give it to me.'

'But it's fastened round my father's neck,' she cried, 'and he is sleeping.'

'Nevertheless,' he said, 'you must get it.'

Then, like a phantom figure in a dream, she glided into her father's room, unclasped the golden key from round his neck and gave it to her suitor. Light as a leaf he darted to the sluice-gate and unlocked it. At once the inky waters began leaking in, stealing over the streets and avenues, swirling into the courtyards, engulfing the milky fountains and submerging the gardens. Then, gathering speed, the black swell swept through the mansions and houses and began rushing in a torrent towards the church.

From his late office in the sacristy the Abbot Guénolé heard the dark seas rising. He rushed out, plunging through the water, saddled his horse and charged towards the castle, rousing the citizens. But Gradlon was already on his horse with Dahut clinging on behind him. The Abbot saw the king's horse rear and stumble.

'Throw her off!' he shouted, 'Throw the demon off and save yourself!'

As Gradlon hesitated, the Abbot came up to him, reached out with his staff and thrust Dahut into the water. At once the king's horse sprang away, and both the Abbot and the King reached dry land safely. Looking back they watched the water open its jaws like a great black monster and swallow the moon-pearled city. Then they saw the water writhe and boil while the city slid through its great belly and made its way to the bottom of the sea.

The druidess paused and her eyes swept over us.

'And there it lies still,' she said, 'between our shrouded island and the *Bay des Trespasses.* And as the dead pass over, sometimes they hear from underneath the waves the sad-sweet voice of Dahut-Ahes rising up, lamenting her fair city.' (32)

The druidess gazed at us again.

'And that,' she said, 'is the end of Dahut's story. But now I expect you will want to know what happened to her father.'

As we stood unmoving she continued:

At first he went and lived with the Abbot at his monastery. It was at Landevennec, not far from here, as you know. But Gradlon could not settle there. He said it was too close to the sea and that he could hear his daughter's voice, carried on the wind, crying for her lost city. He could not bear it, so he went off into the woods where he found an old druid, and decided to stay with him.

But, soon enough, the Abbot went looking for Gradlon. He found him in a hut beside a spring and the old druid with him. Gradlon begged the Abbot not to harm the druid.

'He is an old man mourning the death of his gods and the old ways of the land,' he said, 'Leave him be.'

'Maybe he knows no better,' said the Abbot, 'but you do. Come back with me to the monastery and live your life in service and prayer to God.'

But Gradlon chose instead to stay with the old druid, and grieve for his daughter. He tended the old man until he died, and not long afterwards he died himself.

The druidess ceased her story and bowed her head while we all stayed silent. Then from behind and all around the rock she sat on came again the unearthly singing. And this time it grew louder and stronger until it seemed to gather everything, the clouds, the sky, the sea and all of the people listening, into one great throbbing resonance, one pure green eye, one pulse.

When we came to ourselves again, darkness lay over the sea, and the druidess was gone.

Notes to Tales of the Celtic Bards

ERIN

CORMAC MAC ART AND THE FAERIE BRANCH

Bruach is an Irish seer, known as a *fili* (see Introduction).

Cormac mac Art was High King at Tara and ruled in the third century CE. The description of his court at Tara, the sacred place of the High King, is confirmed by archaeological findings. Cormac's wisdom was considered as great as Solomon's. He is credited with devising many of the Brehon Laws known as the *Senchus Mor* (recorded in The Book of the Dun Cow), which were revised every three years at the Assembly at Tara (see Introduction). The purpose of this tale is to suggest that his wisdom was of spiritual origin. Interestingly, however, it is recorded that Cormac disappeared for seven months in the year 284, which was presumably when he visited the Otherworld.

Cormac's daughter was the famous Grainne who later became betrothed to Finn mac Cumhail. In some versions of this story Cormac's daughter is named Ailbe, but it may be that the two daughters are one and the same. The fact that Grainne later demonstrates her druidic wisdom suggests that it was she who journeyed to the Otherworld and drank from the Well of Wisdom (see 'The Love Story of Diarmaid and Grainne').

THE MAGICAL GIFTS OF THE TUATHA DE DANANN

The Tuatha de Danann, the 'People of the Goddess Danu' came 'like a mist' over the water and overcame the giant races, the Firbolgs and Formorians, who inhabited Ireland at that time. The Tuatha were a magical people who brought sacred gifts with them. When the Tuatha were finally defeated by the Milesian race, they were allowed to retreat into the realm below the earth and inhabit the tumuli or burial mounds. From this point onwards they were known as the *sidhe*, or faerie people, who lived on the fringes of the mortal world.

This tale gives the origin of the four mystical objects brought to Ireland by the Tuatha. The Dagda or 'Good God' was their chief deity. His Cauldron of Plenty could nourish men perpetually and also restore dead warriors to life. It is the original sacred cauldron in Celtic myth. Lugh was the Celtic sun god and Nuada was the first king of the Tuatha de Danann, whose sword was said to be inescapable. He became known as Nuada of the Silver Hand because he lost a hand in the First Battle of Magh Tuiredh and had it replaced by an artificial one.

The four sacred objects are linked with the four elements, the four seasons and the four directions. They are potent symbols and reappear in later mystical traditions. For example, the spear and the cauldron became the famous lance and Holy Grail of Arthurian legend, and the sword reappears as Excalibur. (It is interesting to note that Arthur had to lift it from a stone in order to become king). In mediaeval times the four symbols became the four humours and also the basis of the four suits in the tarot deck. According to tradition, the original Stone of Destiny, the *Lia fail*, still survives. It was lent to the king of Scotland in the sixth century CE and is now known as the Stone of Scone.

The Three Noble Strains

The palace of Aengus Og stood beside the River Boyne at Newgrange in Ireland, the site of the famous Neolithic passage tomb.

Boann's other husbands were Elcmar and Nechtan. In this story she gives birth to music in its three moods. Of these three, the *suantrai* or sleep-strain seems to be most prevalent in Irish Myth. For example, in the story of King Cormac mac Art, the music made by the silver branch lulls the citizens into a state of forgetfulness.

The magnificence of a bard's harp denoted his status. The detailed description of the harps of the sons of Boann indicates the godlike status of their owners.

The Birth of Cuchulainn

Conchobar mac Nesa was king of Ulster throughout the life of Cuchulainn. He famously kept a druid at his court, called Cathbad. In the tales of Cuchulainn and the Red Branch heroes Conchobar is portrayed as a just and fair king, but in the tale of Deirdre, he is seen as vengeful and treacherous and loses the support of Cathbad and of Fergus mac Roth, chief of the Red Branch Warriors. Emain Macha was the seat of the Ulster Kings and was named after the horse-goddess Macha. Known today as Navan Fort, it lies two miles west of Armagh.

The first of Cuchulainn's strange 'triple-births' takes place at the magical Brugh na Boyne, site of Aengus Og's palace and the great passage tomb and burial mound of Newgrange. This passage tomb is so constructed that every year on the winter solstice (21st December) the first rays of the sun strike through a special aperture and illumine the inner chamber. The Winter Solstice marked the rebirth of the sacred sun-child. It is therefore no accident that Cuchulainn, the solar hero and son of the sun-god Lugh, should be born at the Brugh.

The two foals that were born at the same time as Cuchulainn remained with him all his life. They were called the Black of Saingliu and the Grey of Macha, and when he reached manhood they pulled his chariot.

Lugh of the Shining Face

Son of the Dagda, Lugh was guardian of the second sacred object brought by the Tuatha, the fiery spear. He was also known as the New God and gradually took over from his father, being equally multi-skilled. Ogma was the god of eloquence and gave his name to the Ogham script (see Introduction). For Nuada – see notes to The Magical Gifts of the Tuatha de Danann.

How Cuchulainn came by his Name

Cuchulainn shows great prowess from a young age and exhibits godlike qualities. Like the Welsh Lleu Llaw Gyffes, he discovers his identity and therefore his name, through his deeds. The prowess demonstrated by Cuchulainn in opposing the hound is both an initiation test and an encounter with his totem animal. When Cuchulainn takes on the role of the hound he has killed, he also takes on its name and thereafter is forbidden to eat dog flesh. The interchanging of a hero with his totem beast was even more intimate than the shamanic practice of shapechanging. By pitting themselves against such beasts, the warriors took on the nature and ferocity of their particular animal, and when their powers failed so, too, did the powers of the animal. The two foals that are born simultaneously with Cuchulainn also have a totem connection with him.

It is not surprising that Conchobar and his retinue went to dine with Culann, for blacksmiths were held in very high regard by the Celts. Their art was considered to be divinely inspired. They were seen as magicians who could bend the element of fire to their will and forge magic weapons.

Cuchulainn's Wooing of Emer

Cuchulainn's skills are not just those of the warrior but also of the seer, and his choice of wife reflects this. He engages Emer in the dark and riddling speech of the trained druid and she responds in the same language. She also prophetically predicts the trials he must overcome in winning her. The encounter between the two is therefore shown as being on many levels. Samhain was the Celtic festival held at the beginning of winter on 1 November. Imbolc was held on 1 February and heralded spring. The Feast of Lugh, or Lughnasagh was held on 1` August and marked the beginning of autumn.

Cuchulainn's Training in Arms

In order to win the love of woman, the hero must prove his worth. Emer's father typically makes the challenge that moves Cuchulainn on to this next stage in his development. Warrior women like Scathach were not uncommon in Celtic times since women were able to receive military training. Scathach's prophecy comes from the original text of the story. In some accounts, Cuchulainn initially rejects Uathach's advances until she places a *geis* on him to become her lover.

The Pillow-talk

'Maeve' means 'the intoxicating one' which suggests that she is alluring and sexual. She uses her sexuality as a powerful tool in negotiation. The offer of her 'friendly thighs' is sufficient to cause the chieftain Daire to jump up and down and burst his cushion, and to keep the virile Ulster warrior Fergus mac Roth firmly in her camp.

Celtic women who owned property were allowed to keep hold of it after marriage. This enabled them to maintain equality with their husbands, so it is not surprising that Maeve is so concerned about the balance of property between herself and Ailill. In order to maintain her regal power, she has deliberately chosen a man who will not overshadow her in wealth and who will tolerate her sexual freedom.

Cuchulainn and Edarcomhol

This tale shows Cuchulainn's military finesse, and also the conflict of honour between his desire to avenge insult and his bond with Fergus. The bond between a child and his foster-father was often stronger than with his natural father and Cuchulainn's greeting of Fergus and acceptance of his punishment shows the love and regard he has for him. Ailill usually allowed Maeve to offer her 'friendly thighs' in order to secure the good of the kingdom - and the securing of Fergus the Ulster warrior was certainly a great boost to Connaught. But the fact that Fergus was famously endowed not only with great military prowess but also with great sexual powers probably accounts for Ailill's jealousy. The stealing of his sword is, of course, symbolic in this respect. Although Fergus is sent as messenger to his foster-son he is careful to preserve his new allegiance to Medbh. Fergus defected to Connacht after King Conchobor's treacherous slaying of the Sons of Usna.

Cuchulainn and the Morrigan

Cuchulainn's encounter with the goddess of war comes at a

critical point when he is worn down by defending Ulster single-handed and his strength is giving out. Through his discourtesy in rejecting her sexual favours, he deprives himself of much needed aid and instead incurs her wrath. His downfall could be said to begin from this point and also indicates the dangers of dishonouring a goddess. The fact that the Morrigan was subject to the wounds he inflicted on her until they were lifted by his blessing is indicative of the hero's godlike attributes.

The Death of Cuchulainn

This story is shot through with symbolic omens. As a flock of birds predicted Cuchulainn's birth, his failure to shoot them is indicative of his approaching death. He has two powerful female enemies, namely Medbh who rears the three daughters of Calatin, and the Morrigan herself. His flouting of such women can be seen as a form of hubris and a rejection of feminine power. In this respect he also rejects the pleading of the Ulster women and the advice of the druid Cathbad. He becomes subject to magical delusions and begins to break his *geis* when obliged to eat dog-flesh.

The idea of *geis* is found throughout Celtic myth. It seems every hero was born with a set of magical restrictions to which he was subject throughout his life. The breaking of his *geasa* signalled his approaching death. It seems that a *geis* could be laid on a person during his lifetime, but only by someone who had supernatural or druidic powers.

The Washer at the Ford is a manifestation of the

Morrigan. The deaths of his charioteer and his totem horse, the Grey of Macha, represent the failing of his own inner powers. At the end, the Morrigan perches on Cuchulainn's shoulder in the guise of a raven, symbolizing his death.

NIALL AND THE GODDESS OF SOVEREIGNTY

The idea of the transformation of the Crone into the Spring Maiden runs deep in Celtic legend, as does the recognition of her sovereignty. This tale appears again in the Arthurian story of 'Gawain and the Lady Ragnell' and also in Chaucer's 'Wife of Bath's Tale'. The Celtic view of kingship was that of the king wedded to the land, and this story ably demonstrates this concept.

FINN AND THE SALMON OF WISDOM

The Well of Wisdom was the primary Celtic source of spiritual understanding and poetic inspiration. It is interesting to note that prowess alone was not considered sufficient for the hero; he was also required to be adept in Otherworldly powers. This story tells how the great warrior Finn was sent as a young boy to be trained in the druidic arts by Finnegas, the seer. The other great Irish hero, Cuchulainn, was also instructed in druidic arts, and was made to study poetry, prophecy and wise judgement alongside his military skills. May-time is an ancient Irish poem.

Oisin goes to the Land of Youth

Although the theme is of ancient origin, the fullest version of this story is found in the eighteenth-century poem by Michael Comyn. Oisin means 'Little Faun' because his mother was both woman and faun. White horses are usually magical and linked with the Otherworld.

The Coming of Adzed Head

The preservation of Oisin for three hundred years allows him to enter into dialogue with St. Patrick and defend the conduct of his Fenian comrades. Oisin then regales Patrick with the old tales of the Fianna, and Patrick finds himself so interested that he fears this might be disrespectful to his Christian religion. He prays to his two guardian angels, asking if he should stop listening to these stories. They answer in one voice that he should make sure the tales are preserved for generations to come. (In 'The Colloquy of the Ancients', it is Cailte, not Oisin, who regales St. Patrick with the old tales.)

ALBA

Harpers on the Island of Rum

This tale has been used as a basis for this whole section. It comes from the Hebrides and was collected by Kenneth MacLeod. The harp, known in Scotland as the clarsach, has long been recognized as both a spiritual and faerie instrument, capable of transporting listeners from one realm to another.

The Ballad of Tam Lin

This is a reworking of the famous ballad collected by Professor Child from James Nicol. Unlike Thomas Rhymer, Tam Lin has not taken steps to defend himself from the magical bindings to Fairyland and fears he will be given to the Devil as the faerie tithe. Having been lured there by the power of a woman, he needs a woman to release him. Significantly, his rescue takes place at Halloween, the night when the veil between the mortal and spirit worlds was traditionally believed to be at its thinnest.

The Sea Maiden

This tale comes from the Shetlands where a creature called the sea-trow was believed to be able to remove its skin after which it could walk on land in mortal shape. The selchie is another example of this, being half-human and half-seal and able to change from one to the other.

The Tale of Thomas the Rhymer

This story is the subject of a famous ballad collected by Child from Mrs. Brown of Falkland. It is based on a historical character, Thomas of Ercildoune, a thirteenth century Scottish laird whose book of prophecies was published in the fifteenth century. Mystically it tells of a journey to the Otherworld. The three taboos - physical contact with a faerie, eating fairie food and speaking to faerie people, would bind him to Faerieland forever. But Thomas is able to return home because he only breaks the first taboo. Nevertheless he is changed by his experience and cannot finally let go. The motif of the faerie apples echoes the 'forbidden fruit' of the Garden of Eden.

THE LOVE STORY OF DIARMAID AND GRAINNE

This powerful triangular love story reflects the Celtic idea of an annual seasonal ritual in which the two great kings of winter and summer, do battle for the hand of the spring goddess. Thus it is inevitable that Finn, the older king, is fated to be overcome by the younger warrior. Grainne's ability to lay a geis on Diarmaid and her riddling exchange with Finn suggest that she possesses druidic powers. (For *geis* see notes to The Death of Cuchulainn.) This lends credence to the idea that she was once taken to the Otherworld (see 'Cormac mac Art and the Faerie Branch').

Diarmaid also has Otherworldly powers, not least the love-spot, which was conferred on him by an Otherworldly woman. He is also fostered by Aengus, the god of love, with whom he seems to have a special relationship. His fate is therefore bound up with the power of love. It is also bound up with the boar, which is his totem animal.

Sallows are willow trees, and *fidchell* is an early form of chess. The

Quicken Tree is a symbol of new life, and the killing of the giant represents the necessary destruction of the old order. Although the death of Diarmaid is said to have taken place on the mountain of Benn Bulben in County Sligo, in Scottish tradition it took place on the ridge between Oban and Loch Awe. The lament for Diarmuid comes from the Irish text for the story.

CYMRU

Pwyll and the Lord of Annwn

Arawn, ruler of Annwn, was also linked with Herne the Hunter, leader of the wild hunt, and Cernunnos, the antler-headed Lord of the Beasts.

Hafgan means 'Summer Song'. This encounter suggests the seasonal conflict between the winter and summer kings and the contest for the hand of the maiden.

In the original text, once he has entered Annwn, Pwyll is no longer referred to by name, but only as 'the man who was in Arawn's stead,' indicating that he is not just Arawn's substitute, but his successor.

Some of the themes from this story also appear in the mediaeval poem 'Gawain and the Green Knight'.

Gwydion's Story, Arianrhod's Story and Flowerbride

This three-part tale is entitled 'Math, son of Mathonwy,' and forms the fourth branch of the *Mabinogi.* Much of the story appears to rest on the misunderstanding between matriarchal and patriarchal modes of thinking. Yet the three women in the story are clearly linked with the land, and the curious idea of the virgin footholder seems to refer to this. Together the three women symbolize the triple-aspects of the goddess - Virgin, Mother and Crone.

Arianrhod means 'silver wheel' and relates to the night sky and moon. In her role as the challenging Goddess, Arianrhod seeks to bestow on her son three tests of initiation. It is Gwydion's misunderstanding of these three 'pledges of destiny' that makes them appear like curses.

Besides the motif of the triple-goddess, at the heart of this story lies the fostering of the sacred king-child. And, although Gwydion and Arianrhod appear to be contending over him, they are, at a deeper level, colluding in his destiny. Lleu's destiny is to become the sacrificial king whose death and resurrection on the World Tree (known as *Yggdrasil* in Norse mythology) is related to the land. Lleu has been linked with Lugh, the Irish god of light, and here, like Lugh, he wields a magic spear of unerring aim.

The killing of Lleu by Gronwy and, afterwards, of Gronwy by Lleu symbolizes the seasonal combat between two rival kings for the hand of the spring maiden.

The hunting of the wren was an ancient Celtic custom undertaken at the time of the winter solstice and therefore symbolizing the ritual sacrifice of the king.

Buried in this myth, too, are the three levels of druidic training - those of bard, vate, and druid. When Gwydion travels to Pryderi's court and entertains the host, he demonstrates his mastery of the bardic art. When he shape-changes into wild animals, he undergoes the shamanic training of the seer. And when he restores life to Lleu through the agency of poetry, he demonstrates his command of full druidic powers.

SONG OF THE SHAMAN

This poem has been inspired by Gwydion's three-fold path of initiation outlined above.

TALIESIN, THE SHINING CHILD

This legendary bard is associated with a historical Taliesin who was Court bard to King Urien Rheged in the sixth century. He also has connections with the seer Myrddin (Merlin). The great Celtic goddess Ceridwen has been variously called the Great Witch, the White Sow and the Dear One. She belongs to the tradition of Scottish Mountain Mothers or Cailleachs. The cauldron is a symbol of regeneration and inspiration. Its three drops carry the same charge as the Salmon of Wisdom. The transformations undergone by Gwion when chased by Ceridwen are of an initiatory and shamanic nature. Like Arianrhod, Ceridwen is a challenger who also becomes the mother of the bard. When he appears to Elphin in place of the salmon catch, he symbolizes the Salmon of Wisdom itself. Taliesin means 'Shining Child' and the child shines with Otherworldly and inspirational knowledge. His inspired poetry springs from his shamanic and Otherworldly experiences. In the original text, the story of Taliesin is interspersed with a folk tale concerning the testing of the chastity of Elphin's wife. In this retelling the folkloric elements have been omitted.

ARMORICA

THE CITY OF YS

This tale is set in the fifth century CE and reflects the conflict between paganism and Christianity. King Gradlon, known as Gradlon Meur, is a historical figure who converted to Christianity and appointed Corentin as bishop of Quimper. The city of Ys is believed to lie beneath the sea – either off the coast of the Pointe du Raz or at the end of the causeway of Penmarc'h.

Dahut has evidently been demonized by Christian writers. As the daughter of a mermaid, she represents the old matriarchal religion, symbolized by the sea. With their mirrors and combs, mermaids were regarded by the Church as the epitome of female vanity. They were considered dangerous yet alluring creatures, capable of leading men to their doom.

The 'Island of the Blessed' is the *Isle de Seine* off the west coast of Brittany, which was anciently believed to be inhabited by nine druidesses who tended the souls of the dead. The number nine was often used for groups of Otherworldly women in Celtic myth, and denoted great power. As receivers of dead souls, the druidesses can be seen as representing ancient regenerative matriarchal forces. In his hermit guise, Corentin appears to form a link with the old religion. The miraculous fish is reminiscent of the fabled Salmon of Wisdom.

There is a statue of King Gradlon on horseback between the twin spires of the Cathedral of Quimper in Cornouaille. According to the *Barzaz Breiz,* every year a ritual was enacted on St. Cecile's day in which a minstrel would climb up to the statue, carrying a white napkin, a jug of wine and a golden goblet. He would tie the napkin around the king's neck and present him with the goblet of wine. Then, having drunk the wine himself, he would throw down the goblet to the waiting crowd. This annual ceremony ceased at the time of the French Revolution.

Glossary and Guide to Irish and Welsh Celtic pronunciation

As a general guide to Welsh pronunciation, *ll* sounds *cl* or *chl*; *dh* sounds *th*, as in 'then'; *ch* and *gh* are guttural.

In Irish pronunciation *b* sounds *v*; *c* sounds *g* or *k*; *ch* is guttural, *d* sounds *dh*, as in 'then' (represented below as *dh*); *g* is a soft guttural and sounds *gh*; *m* sounds *v*; *t* sounds *d*. *s* with either i or e before or after it, is pronounced *sh*; *th* is pronounced softly as in 'thin'; *ai* is pronounced as *a*; *ei* is pronounced as *e*.

Aengus Og	*Angus Og* (as in Ogre) son of Boanne and the Dagda. God of love
Ailill	*Alil* – king of Connacht and husband of Queen Medbh
Alba	Scotland
Amargin	*Avarghin* – Ulster warrior. Tutor to Cuchulainn
Annwn	*Anoon* – name of Celtic Underworld or Otherworld
Arianrhod	*Arianrod* – sister of Gwydion, mother of Lleu Llaw Gyffes
Avagddu	*Av-ugdhi* – misshapen son of Welsh goddess, Ceridwen

Beltain	Celtic May Day Festival
Blodeuwedd	*Blod-eye-wedh* – wife made out of flowers for Lleu
Boann	Mother of Aengus mac Og, gave name to Boyne
Bricriu	Known as 'the Poison-tongued', Ulster hero, mischief-maker
Brugh	*Brew* – palace of Aengus Og beside the River Boyne. Also the site of the megalithic passage tomb of Newgrange
Cantrev	*Kantrev* – Welsh unit of land, a hundred homesteads
Cathbad	*Kathvadh* – chief Druid to King Conchobar of Ulster
Conchobor	*Kon-ch-ovor* – king of Ulster c. beginning Christian era
Cormac mac Art	Third-century High King of Tara
Cruachan	*Kruakan* – Royal seat of Maeve and Ailill in Connacht, also site of cave entrance to Otherworld
Cuchulainn	*Ku-chull-in* – 'Hound of Culann'. Hero of Ulster cycle
Culann	Ulster warrior chief whose hound was killed by Cuchulainn

Cymru	*Coomree* – Wales
Dagda	Chief god of the Tuatha de Danann
Dahut	*Da-hoot* – daughter of Gradlon, a Breton King
Dechtire	Sister of Conchobar and mother to Cuchulainn
Demna	Original name of Finn mac Cumhail
Diarmaid	*Dermot* – grandson of Duibne (dina), Fenian warrior abductor of Grainne.
Edarcomhol	Foster-son of Medbh and Ailill. Killed by Cuchulainn
Elphin	Welsh Prince who fosters Taliesin
Emain Macha	*Evin Ma-cha* – Capital of Ulster
Emer	*Ay-ver* – Wife of Cuchulainn
Englyn	Welsh verse-form
Fergus mac Roth	Great Ulster hero, defected to Connaught after Conchobor killed the Sons of Usna
Fianna	Organized military band led by Finn mac Cumhail
Finn (Fionn) mac Cumhail	*Fyun m' Cool* – Captain of the Fianna

Forgall	Father of Emer
Geis, geasa	*Gaysh* – magical taboo or prohibition
Gilvaethwy	Gwydion's brother
Goewin	Math's virgin footholder
Grainne	*Graun-yeh* – daughter of Cormac mac Art, wife of Finn, elopes with Diarmuid
Gronwy Pebr	*Gronwi Pevr.* Lover of Blodeuwedd. Kills Lleu Llaw Gyffes
Gwydion	Magician and brother of Arianrhod
Laeg	Cuchulainn's charioteer
Lleu Llaw Gyffes	*Chlay Chlow Geh-feth* – magically birthed son of Arianrhod
Lugh	*Loo* – son of the Dagda, a chief of Tuatha, god of light, father of Cuchulainn
Math	King of Gwynedd, uncle of Gwydion
Manannan	Sea-god, a chief of the Tuatha de Danann
Medbh	*Mave,* Queen of Connaught
Morrigan	Goddess of war
Niall	Known as 'of the Nine Hostages'. Historical Irish king, established fifth province and capital at Tara

Niamh	*Neeve* – faerie woman who lured Oisin to Otherworld
Nuada	First king of Tuatha. Lost his hand in battle, and had a silver one made for him.
Oisin	*Osheen* – fenian warrior, son of Finn
Ogham	*O'am* – cryptic druidic language
Pryderi	Son of Pwyll
Pwyll	*Poochl* – with oo as in 'foot' - Lord of Dyfed who changed places with Arawn, Lord of Annwn
Rath	Fortified dwelling surrounded by wall or ditch
Red Branch	Ulster warrior band
Samhain	*Sowain* – Celtic Festival, now Halloween
Scathach	*Scaw-thach* – female warrior who trained Cuchulainn
Sidhe	*Shee* – faerie, also burial mound or barrow
Slieve	A mountain, or mountainous district
Tain Bo Cuailnge	*Toyn Bo Cooling* – The Cattle Raid of Cooley, central epic of Ulster Cycle
Taliesin	Greatest bard of Wales

Tara	Seat of High Kings of Ireland in County Meath
Torc	*Tawk* – Celtic neck ring denoting high status.
Tir na n'Og	*Teer nan owg* – the Land of Youth, or Otherworld
Tuatha de Danann	*Tooatha day Daanan* – race that conquered Ireland and later dwelt in the faerie mounds
Uaithne	*Ooaythnie* – harper to the Dagda
Ys	*Ees* – drowned city off west coast of Brittany

Select Bibliography

Aubert, O.L., *Celtic Legends of Brittany*, Coop Breizh (Kerangwenn), 1993.

Cross, T. P. and Slover, C. H., *Ancient Irish Tales*, Barnes and Noble, 1936.

Dooley, A. and Row, H. (trans), *Tales of the Elders of Ireland*, OUP, 1999.

Eddie, S. and Hamilton, C., *Timeless Wisdom of the Celts*, Hodder and Stoughton, 1999.

Gantz, Jeffrey (trans), *The Mabinogion*, Penguin, 1976.

Green, Miranda J., *Exploring the World of the Druids*, Thames and Hudson, 1997.

Guest, Lady Charlotte (trans), *The Mabinogion*, Llanerch, 1990.

Hamilton, Claire, *The Celtic Book of Seasonal Meditations*, Rider, 2002.

Hyde, Douglas, *A Literary History of Ireland*, T. Fisher Unwin, 1899.

Jackson, Kenneth Hurlstone (trans.), *A Celtic Miscellany*, Penguin, 1971.

James, Jamie, *The Music of the Spheres*, Abacus, 1993.

Jones, Gwyn and Thomas, *The Mabinogion*, Everyman, 1949.
Kinsella, Thomas (trans.), *The Tain*, OUP, 1969.

Matthews, Caitlin and John, *The Encyclopaedia of Celtic Wisdom*, Element, 1994.

Rolleston, T. W., *Celtic Myths and Legends*, Senate, 1994.